HAWAII
TRUTH STRANGER
THAN FICTION

Other Books by the Author

HAWAII THIS & THAT

HAWAII'S MISSIONARY SAGA

BIG ISLAND HISTORY MAKERS

HAWAII
TRUTH STRANGER THAN FICTION

True Tales of Missionary Life
and Historic Characters Fictionalized in
Michener's epic novel *Hawaii*

by LaRue W. Piercy

Mutual Publishing

ISBN 1-55647-328-4

Cover design by Julie Matsuo

Mass market
First Printing, July 2000
Second Printing, April 2003
2 3 4 5 6 7 8 9

Mutual Publishing
1215 Center Street, Suite 210
Honolulu, Hawaii 96816
Ph: (808) 732-1709
Fax: (808) 734-4094
e-mail: mutual@lava.net
www.mutualpublishing.com

Printed in Australia

DEDICATED TO

The readers of James A. Michener's "Hawaii" to give them greater knowledge and clearer understanding of the true characters, spirit and lives of the real New England missionaries to Hawaii; and to the Hawaiian Mission Children's Society for their preservation of such records.

THANK YOU, READERS

My hearty thanks to all my precious readers over the past five years who have lauded my work as pleasantly informative in an entertaining style. It has given me heartwarming satisfaction to hear their praise of my efforts as I greet them at Mokuaikaua Church or read their approval in their letters

LaRue W. Piercy

CONTENTS

Part One: THE DEVELOPING MISSION

Part Three: SPECIAL PEOPLE, SPECIAL PROBLEMS

Part One
THE DEVELOPING MISSION

I. THE BLEAK SIDE OF RELIGION

"From the Farm of Bitterness" sprouts James Michener's Abner Hale, the sad figure of "a thin, sallow-faced youth with stringy blond hair" leaving "an impoverished-looking farm." No place of joy is poor Abner's home. It is "a bleak unkindly" one. For his parents are bleak and dour. Their farm is one of "penury" with "an austerity of purpose that was positively repellent" except that it was "dedicated to God." The family's single purpose in life is "striving toward salvation."

Religious fervor enthralls the Hales. Abner at the age of 11 has been marked for the ministry after a customary miraculous conversion in the farm fields one evening when a voice from above directs him to seek his salvation. From then on, his pious father devotes his body and soul and his farm to produce sacrificial funds to consecrate his "predestined boy" to the service of God.

♣ ♣ ♣

Religious domination was a fairly accepted way of life in early New England, where, under Puritan ideals, the clergy ruled over the peoples' thoughts and lives. Having rebelled against the forms and dictates of the Church of England, the Separatists endured many hardships to battle their way to the New World to win the religious liberty they demanded. There they set up their own theocracy to regulate peoples' lives by biblical dictates and their own irreconcilable interpretations thereof. With their code of indisputable morals and correct manners derived from their self-determined views of God's rule, the Puritans sometimes went into such extremes as to dominate lives to the point of injustice and even cruelty, establishing "Blue Laws" to enforce their ideas of right and wrong.

But there is no need to scoff at the missionaries' strong concept of God and their duty to Him. They were men and women of their times. Such principles had directed them throughout their lives. They came not from the more tolerant cities of New England nor from such "gracious villages" as Walpole, N.H., home of Michener's more worldly Bromleys, that "bespoke good living rather than piety." The missionaries came from rural places where people rigidly depended on God's favor for their livelihood and well-being and strictly studied and applied the Word of God in church and home life. Their special way of life was sacred to them, and so they could not countenance any other way with differing standards.

II. What's In A Name?

Readers of Michener's "Hawaii" often want to know "Is Hale a missionary name?" or "Which missionary was Michener writing about in the person of Abner Hale?"

None was named Hale. None was really at all like Abner Hale. He is a figment of Michener's imagination and a character designed for his plot.

The "disarming innocence" of Abner Hale may suggest a modern name source—that of another well-known farm lad, the fabulous cartoon character, Li'l Abner and his follies.

🐾 🐾 🐾

The only missionary named Abner was Abner Wilcox with the eighth missionary company. But he, happily, was far from displaying the Hale character. He served most of his career teaching school at Waioli, Kauai. One of the chiefs, Paki, did choose Abner as his Christian name. Of course it is a biblical name, and such names were common among the bible-following Puritans. Abner, Saul's cousin and commander of his army, was a tragic character who met his death at the hand of Joab.

Some visitors insist they have seen the name "Hale" on various signs in the islands. But that is the common Hawaiian word for "house," pronounced "Holl-ay," as Malama did say Abner's name.

🐾 🐾 🐾

Abner's admirable mate also bears a biblical name, Jerusha, which Abner's sister admires. "Isn't that a sweet name?" she remarks. "It was Jotham's mother's name in Kings."

This was also the name of Daniel Chamberlain's wife in the pioneer missionary party.

☙ ☙ ☙

Michener's name for his missionary ship, the *Thetis*, is also fictional in that respect, although in Hawaii's history a British bark by that name did serve in 1852 to bring back 300 Chinese coolies to become contract laborers for the sugar plantations.

The original missionary transporter in 1819 was the *Thaddeus*, and the next ship was the *Thames*.

Michener's missionary company is completely fictional. They leave Boston on September 1, 1821, and land early the next year at Lahaina, Maui, never the original destination of any missionary company. The *Thaddeus* left Boston on October 23, 1819, reached Kailua-Kona April 4, 1820. The *Thames* sailed from New Haven, Conn., November 20, 1822, arriving at Honolulu, April 27, 1823.

III. THE IMPELLING FORCE

The initial role for Keoki Kanakoa in the novel is to set off the emotional bombshell of fiery rhetoric that impels Abner Hale and his Yale roommate John Whipple to offer to sacrifice their lives for the salvation of "those human souls destined for all eternity to everlasting hell" in Owhyhee. Michener makes Keoki a son of high lineage and as such a "young giant 6 feet 5 and weighing more than 250 pounds."

A partial reflection of the true story is the account of his early time in America. He lands at Boston from a whaling ship (although whaling did not get under weigh until later), is laughed at when he wants to study at Harvard (a made up angle), walks to New Haven, and, meeting President Day of Yale College on the street, asserts, "I come seek Jesus." And the accosted president emphatically assures him he has come to the right place.

His views of his homeland are devastating—a place of idol-worshiping, polygamy, immorality, grossness and bestiality—of human sacrifices—of "immortal souls [that] go every night to everlasting hell."

♣ ♣ ♣

Far different and more like a biblical tale is the true life story of this remarkable Hawaiian lad, whose life and death stirred up the widespread inspiration for successive bands of missionaries to forsake their good life in New England to make that long, harsh journey by sea to faraway islands to bring Christ to this lad's neglected land. Events seemed heaven-directed to snatch him away from evil and make an admirable example of him.

Some guiding light saved him alone of his family in the aftermath slaughter of tribal warfare, made him a child of destiny, sent him wandering for a year over vast oceans to strange lands, and finally gave him the guidance of many fine educated and religious families to weld his mind and purpose for the great task of taking home enlightenment for his native people.

Henry Obookiah was the name he became known by, but that was the English spelling of his Hawaiian name, Opukahaia, which for some reason means "ripped belly."

(Such odd appellations seemed to please the Hawaiian sense of association. Chester Lyman found their name giving to be "fanciful & often amusing." He noted, "Lava is Pele's excrement, & many other things are named with a like disregard for delicacy...Children are generally named from some personal mark or from some circumstance. Boki, former governor of Oahu, was named from a dog 'Boss,' that being as near as the natives could pronounce it." A child was named "Four-inch" because the mother's friend "had had a piece 4 inches large cut from her breast. Some are named by such names as 'Little-mouth', 'Big-belly' 'Big-navel' & other names so indelicate & [even] obscene that the missionaries are obliged to refuse to baptize the children by them." Anyway, the name Obookiah in America was simply an odd foreign one.)

The strange story of Opukahaia begins when he was 10 years old, about 1802, living at Ka'u at the southern tip of the Island of Hawaii. Savage battles there had caused Opukahaia's family to try to save themselves by fleeing up on Mauna Loa and hiding in a cave. When thirst drove them out to get water from a spring, pursuing warriors captured them, slaughtered the parents, hurled a spear killing the baby brother when Opukahaia tried to make a getaway with the child on his back.

But Opukahaia was destined not to be sacrificed. Fate stayed the hand of the leader who had murdered the boy's parents. He spared Opukahaia's life, took him home with him and treated him kindly.

Providence continued to pave the way for Opukahaia. Six years later he was serving as an apprentice *kahuna* (native priest) with his uncle at Hikiau Heiau (Temple), conveniently right on the shore of Kealakekua Bay. He too harbored a longing to visit other lands. Then in 1808 the Yankee ship *Triumph* sailed into the bay, captained by Caleb Brintnall of New Haven. Opukahaia swam out to the ship, found on board another Hawaiian boy, Hopu of Kohala, received a hearty welcome from the congenial commander. Captain Brintnall managed to induce Opukahaia's uncle to let the boy travel with him, promising he would treat him as his own son.

Now Opukahaia became Henry Obookiah. A year-long trip of strange sights and adventures gave this 16-year-old youth a marvelous view of the great world beyond—six months at the Seal Islands of North America loading the ship with furs—back to Honolulu, then on to China—rescuing Hopu after he fell overboard and had to battle the waves for two and a half hours—the captain seized by British seamen at Macao but released—selling the sealskins at Canton and reloading with tea, cinnamon, nankeens (heavy cloth for trousers) and silks.

As they were crossing the equator in the Indian Ocean, the terrible Neptune, clad in sheepskins, confronted the boys and frighteningly commanded each boy to draw a bucket of sea water and suck it in through a trumpet. Obookiah proved his cleverness by sticking the end of the trumpet in his cheek and just pretending to drink. Hapless Hopu was not so smart. He artlessly swallowed the salty drink and, as Obookiah relates, "puked all the next day."

They rounded Cape of Good Hope, almost ran out of food, but got some provisions from a passing schooner in the Atlantic, reached New York in 1809, sold the Chinese goods, and arrived at home port in New Haven. Captain Brintnall took Obookiah into his home there.

Obookiah's education had started aboard the *Triumph* with a spelling book and instruction from a Russell Hubbard, a Yale student member of the crew. During his next nine years in New England, he lived with various families and worked on farms in Connecticut, Massachusetts and New Hampshire.

The heart-warming tale of his anxious yearning for education pictures him weeping late one day on the steps of Yale College "because nobody gives me learning." There a Yale student, Edwin W. Dwight, comforts him and shares his quarters with him, and, with the help of fellow students, leads him along the path of knowledge. Obookiah's guardian angel had things going right. Edwin's father was Dr. Timothy Dwight, president of Yale, who then took Obookiah under his wing "for a season." Here this Hawaiian boy found himself in a "praying family morning and evening."

It was at Yale that Samuel J. Mills, promoter of the missionary cause, met Obookiah, took a strong interest in him and conceived the plan of making this Hawaiian youth the foundation for the Sandwich Islands Mission. Obookiah spent much of his time then on the Mills farm at Torringford, Conn., with the elder Mills, the local minister, and with the son and his student friends at Andover Seminary.

During all this shifting around, Obookiah's religious development was an up and down struggle. Though he accepted repetitious praying at the Timothy Dwight household, he did not seem able to fit the worship of God into his way of life yet. While working on a farm where deacons and ministers often discussed the ways and works of God quite familiarly, he claimed he did not feel comfortable with such divine discourse. He figured he was "just as happy as other people who do not know God much more than I do." But later, with Mills and the Andover students, he did begin to feel more understanding of God. Then he attended Bradford Academy and felt that there he lost his "serious feelings" about religion and let himself frisk with his carefree classmates.

Back at Andover, while working on a nearby farm, Obookiah reports he heard voices. "I fell upon my knees and looked up to the Almighty Jehovah for help. I was not but an undone and hell-deserving sinner." During the following two years he became increasingly religious as he studied the scriptures.

His future career was beginning to shape up. Young Mills, after being ordained, baptized him, the first known Hawaiian to receive this sacrament. Obookiah joined the church at Goshen, Conn., in 1815. Then he came under the care of the recently organized American Board of Commissioners for Foreign Missions (ABCFM) "to be a missionary to my poor countrymen," as he felt for them the "loss of their souls."

It was at the close of 1816 that Obookiah was taken to Amherst on a tour to solicit donations for the Foreign Mission School about to be established. An inspirational speaker, he was not the inciting dramatic type of Keoki Kanakoa to drive his listeners into instant action. It was his simple humble sincerity that impressed the people, for his simple talks were "always appropriate, solemn, and interesting." He was effective enough that the contributions to the school were "highly liberal."

His great value to the growing missionary cause was that he clearly demonstrated that the "heathen" were not "too ignorant to be taught," thus silencing the opposition to such foreign undertakings on that score. Many self-righteous church members had remained hesitant to contribute to such a far-off project of soul salvation because they felt that such wild creatures could not be Christianized, being already condemned victims of Satan. But now the interest in foreign missions started to spread.

In Obookiah the missionary promoters found a native man, converted, intelligent, inspired, devoted and determined, well-primed to take the field for Jesus Christ in his benighted Owhyhee. They opened the Foreign Mission School at Cornwall, Conn., in May, 1817. This would provide education and specialized missionary training for Obookiah, Hopu, five other Hawaiian boys, one Bengalese, one Hindu, one Indian, and two Anglo-Americans.

Obookiah was already working on educational tools for teaching his unlearned countrymen, preparing a spelling book, dictionary, and grammar for his native language. He also was translating Genesis into Hawaiian, using the Hebrew text because he found that language more like his own than English.

Mills, the ABCFM, and other mission leaders delighted in the way the Lord had provided such a natural opportunity for their converting of those heathen Hawaiians. But they knew not the way of the Lord. It was a shock to them when Obookiah succumbed to typhus fever early in 1818 and died.

But the spiritual rebound from that tragic circumstance was the true divine inspiration that was to make the Sandwich Island Mission the greatly rewarding success it became. Those who had thrilled at the thought of Obookiah becoming the savior of his poor people, and those who read this pathetic story in the "Memoirs" that Edwin Dwight published, felt driven to take up the cross and carry on the crusade denied this native youth. Volunteers came forward just as eagerly and determinedly as did Abner Hale and John Whipple in response to Kanakoa's igniting outburst.

IV. The Real Missionaries

True to the actual source of missionary training, Abner Hale does follow his studies at Yale College. Though it cost his penurious father more to send his dedicated son a hundred miles farther to the south than to nearby Harvard, Gideon Hale must avoid at all costs having his boy "contaminated in such a den of iniquitousness" by the evil ideas of "Unitraians, deists and atheists." So Abner is to "glorify God" by learning "the honest if austere precepts of John Calvin as expressed in New England Congregationalism" at safe, conservative Yale.

♠ ♠ ♠

The ministerial leaders of the pioneer company were two farm boys. Hiram Bingham, who was in charge and developed the mission in Honolulu, was from Bennington, Vt., while Asa Thurston, who was to take over the first mission at Kailua, came from Fitchburg, Mass. They had typical biblical first names, those of Hiram, king of Tyre, and Asa, king of Judah.

Hiram Bingham's farmer father was undoubtedly a sincerely religious man but evidently not so heavenly bent as to aim to devote his all to supporting higher educational ambitions for his son. Like other farmers' sons, Hiram therefore expected to follow in his father's footsteps, even considering farm lands in the pioneer states to the west of New England.

But the power of the Lord seems to have influenced his thoughts and intentions until he finally determined to learn where more education might lead him. He felt he should then "watch the dealings of providence." He must have been working and saving for his education, occasionally teaching school during the workless farm days of winter. He was 22 by the time he finally entered Middlebury College.

His father, had he any compunctions about his son's going to sinful Harvard, could well approve of Middlebury as a safe haven. The College well served Hiram's ambitions and likewise provided a thorough Calvinistic foundation. For Middlebury was one of Yale's offsprings. Its founders had been proteges of Yale President Timothy Dwight, and its first president was a Yale graduate.

It was a suitable place for farm boys inspired by a craving for higher learning to work their way through college. Tuition in those times was low—a mere $18 a term at Amherst, for instance. The high cost might be health, as poor boys tried to manage to get along on almost nothing, perhaps then leaving them a life of aches and pains and general weakness later. It was thus that poor Abner Hale had to subsist on meager sustenance, until, in his senior year, he was "emaciated."

Asa Thurston's early life had none of that severe austerity. Certainly no bleakness marred his happy home. His family were acclaimed by their fellow townspeople of Fitchburg as the "gay singing Thurstons." Asa's father had taught singing schools in nearby towns, and Asa's mother had been one of his most charming, sweet-voiced pupils at Concord, Mass. At Fitchburg, his father led the church choir for over 30 years.

Though part of a naturally religious family, Asa was a fun-loving young boy not bothered by God-fearing thoughts to interfere with his spontaneous love of sport and good times. He romped with his boyhood companions, wrestled them to the ground, and won their admiration by being able to perform the difficult feat of leaping into and out of a hogshead without ever touching the sides.

Local religious restraints at that period did not eliminate the pleasure of an occasional warming beverage. The minister enjoyed calling on his Thurston parishioners, for, it is reported, he there "found a welcome to their hospitality, and…the old-fashioned courtesy of the best flip (a spicy, sweet drink of ale or beer, sometimes with beaten egg) was ready for his lips."

Nor was that often-blamed pastime of dancing pro-hibited in town social circles. Asa became the life of the party at ballroom dances, such affairs being considered tame without his lively participation. Asa sometimes thought of religion as something to turn to in the future to secure him a place in heaven, but he was loathe to heed the warnings of his more restrained friends and of his sister to "forsake your beloved sinful companions and repent, turning to God and holiness." Instead, he still delighted in being the "gayest of the gay."

His eventual conversion was far different from Abner's boyhood overpowering experience in the farm fields. Tragedy struck his happy home. Typhoid fever raged through the town, and even Asa's stalwart constitution succumbed to the dread disease. He wavered on the threshold of death, as his loving mother nursed him. Then he recovered. But his dear mother fell a fatal victim, his brother Thomas died soon after, and next his devoted sister Elizabeth was destroyed by the disease.

Left in despair, Asa sought relief in the earnest reli-gious zeal of the orthodox dogmas and doctrines of the new church in Fitchburg. As his dying brother Thomas, who had already pledged his life to God and the ministry, had implored Asa to take up such service in his place, Asa at 22 turned his efforts to preparing himself to manifest his newly acquired faith.

With such convictions and determination, Asa prepared for college and, with careful religious consideration, selected Yale. To reach New Haven from Fitchburg in those days required 10 or 15 days of travel. At Yale Asa's athletic prowess won favorable recognition. Being no fragile freshman, he was not one to submit to the rough hazing by sophomores. The faculty realized his potentials. When they learned the sophs were plotting their mischief, they sent Asa up to subdue them. He did the job.

Asa and Hiram went on to Andover Seminary in 1816 for three years of training for their ministry.

V. Finding Females—Or How To Get A Wife In A Hurry

It came as an unexpected blow to unsophisticated Abner "that the Board will send no minister abroad who is not married." He felt he had no need for a wife; he "had learned to sew and cook..." He did not even know "some dedicated young female"—or any female at all.

But the Reverend Thorn has his sly plot to get Abner married to his lovely niece, Jerusha Bromley, deserted for three years by her sailor lover and now "in love with God and self-punishment on some distant island."

Nine of Abner's companions get married, as he does, in "abruptly arranged" weddings promoted by friends who could recommend "unmarried girls of piety." These unions had to be made so spontaneously that those nine aspiring bridegrooms had no more time to get acquainted with their lifetime partners than "four days before banns were announced." Even after saying their vows, Abner and

Jerusha and five other couples still felt such strangers that they dared not address each other by their first names.

Though Michener claims that none of the other "amorous odysseys was stranger than the one conducted by Abner Hale," the fortuitous arrangements of fate or the hand of God truly worked out in the odd love stories of the real missionaries seem none the less remarkable.

♠ ♠ ♠

It was the very wisdom of the American Board of Commissioners for Foreign Missions (ABCFM), directors of the mission program, that sent the eager mission candidates scrambling for altar partners. The Board members harbored natural fears that the devoted religious lives of their men might by unduly hampered by life in a modern Eden where so many Eves offered temptations. Such doubts arose from tales about those who did return and of those who preferred to stay and indulge in such enjoyments. Thus, as Michener states, the Board decided "to require even young men who lived in a state of grace to take their converted women with them."

Wedded to their religious aspirations and void of feminine companionship at their men-only schools, the incipient missionaries were scarcely prepared with marital prospects to satisfy such a demand for female partners in their missionary endeavors. Though these desperate young men sometimes met early failures, friends sometimes came to their rescue by recommending suitable females.

"Girls of known piety" were the goals of these men seeking to win the proper partner willing to forsake family and friends to join earnestly in such an amazing and demanding adventure. This was still true a decade later when Connecticut-born David Lyman, like Abner the dedicated son of a farmer with "slender resources," haply discovered in Boston Sarah Joiner of Vermont, a girl with "overpowering religious fervor." Their son Henry, in recounting their missionary lives, explains that at that time "there was scarcely any outlet for the energies of young people except through church work and religious extension in foreign lands."

Immersed mainly in thoughts of holy matters, though not including matrimony, the six bachelors the Board accepted now set about seeking the needed helpmates. Three met no difficulty in their quest, but the other three of these determined bride-seekers faced uncertainties.

The youngest of the pioneer group, 19-year-old Elisha Loomis, his appointment by the Board at long last confirmed, was hurrying homeward from the Foreign Mission School at Cornwall, Conn., to Rushville, N.Y. Avoiding travel on the holy Sabbath, he stopped at Utica. And there, lo and behold, "as a particular interposition of Divine Providence," he discovered a worthy female long yearning "to engage in a Mission." Maria Sartwell, a former teacher, was working in the printing plant that Elisha visited. With such knowledge of Elisha's occupational interest and "skilled in household arts," she made a most fitting partner for Elisha, aiming to go as the mission's printer.

Quite unlike scrawny young Abner, the two leaders of this mission were fine specimens of manhood. Hiram Bingham was a rather handsome young man, intelligent, self-confident and charming. Such attractions seem to have helped pave the way for him with a girl named Sarah, a minister's daughter, who also felt some urge for saving heathen souls. Hiram confidently waited three months for her acceptance of his proposal, but she and her parents finally decided that was asking too much to take her away forever to struggle through life among those savages.

Though the Lord seemed to have failed Hiram in this particular need, he took this disappointment, as he would many others in the future, as a mark of God's testing his faith. True friends came to his aid with the names of other pious females missionary-inclined, but time was now too late for busy Hiram to go wandering about searching. He left it to the Lord to provide.

And God did not let him down. It was now time for his ordination, September 29, at the small town of Goshen, Conn., crowded with guests to witness this big event. A late arrival was Sybil Moseley, all the way from Canandaigua, N.Y. It was from there that Elisha Loomis, the young printer, had responded to the sad fate of Obookiah and the pressing need of the youth's native land for missionaries. Elisha's noble action had so prompted her own desires for participation in this great work that she had journeyed to Connecticut to applaud the two leaders about to be made ministers of the gospel.

As Divine Providence would have it, she with her minister happened to be received at the parsonage by ailing
Hiram, suffering from weariness and sore throat. So it
fell to his lot to escort them to a deacon's home for accommodations.

Learning next day that this Miss Moseley was indeed
one of the devoted young ladies previously suggested by
his friends, Hiram lost no time in linking her dedication
to the Lord's purposes to his own. As their forceful desires to serve God and save heathen souls so nicely coin-
cided, they were married October 11 at Hartford, less
than two weeks before their departure for their foreign
mission field.

Asa Thurston also experienced an initial rejection
somewhat similar to Bingham's. A long-time social favorite, he was already engaged to a girl perfectly willing
to go with him to the ends of the world. But her mother's
strenuous objections to such a separation forced her to
give up her lover and his far-flung adventure scheme.
Brokenhearted, the girl fell ill and died. Her mother
followed her to the grave a few months after.

A fresh hope came to Asa from one of his Andover
classmates. William Goodell suggested his cousin, Lucy
Goodale (people then did not care whether they spelled
their names differently), a school teacher. Her father
was Abner—Deacon Abner Goodale of Marlboro, Mass.
The name of Abner Hale's hometown is now Hudson,
Mass., north of present-day Marlboro.

William visited his cousin, and she agreed to talk with Asa about the prospect of a common future for them. This was September 23, just a week before his ordination, that Asa traveled to Marlboro for the interview. He was received not just by Lucy but by her father, her two brothers and their wives, and William Goodell's father.

When this family conclave finally left the wondering couple alone, they engaged in serious conversation and parted at midnight "interested friends." In her room upstairs, Lucy paced the floor, weighing the circumstances, and finally reaching her decision. Next morning Asa and Lucy pledged themselves to become "close companions in the race of life." Charming Asa had won the first convert to his cause, a lovely girl, eight years younger than he, but with the same long-suffering devotion to the great Christian endeavor they were about to undertake.

That such lovely girls should be allowed to be carted off so dreadfully far away to lead such dangerous and toilsome lives removed from the comforts of civilization, or, as Bingham put it, "to live or die among the barbarians," seemed appalling to many who opposed taking women on such a mission. As one man declared, after gazing at the glorious beauty of Betsey, destined to suffer a brief career later as the wife of missionary Lorenzo Lyons, "That one oughter not go. She's too purty. Them savages'll EAT her!"

Yet requiring a wife to go with each man proved to be not only for the husband's moral protection but a most important asset for winning acceptance, approval, admiration and refinement among the natives, who rarely before had beheld a white woman.

The other three bachelors met fewer obstacles in their paths to winning acceptable and accepting partners. Friends of Samuel Whitney put him in touch with Mercy Partridge of Pittsfield, Mass. Samuel Ruggles experienced no difficulty in finding and winning Nancy Wells of East Windsor, Conn. And Dr. Thomas Holman and Ruggles' sister Lucia were already deeply in love, just waiting for the means to get married.

Daniel Chamberlain already had a wife (and her name was Jerusha) and five children. These seven couples made up that first company to venture forth on the Sandwich Islands Mission.

VI. SETTING GLORIOUS GOALS

"Tall, god-like Eliphalet Thorn" in the novel delivers the Board's glorious instructions to his group of 22 sacrificing souls. His tongue-rolling first name is unmistakably biblical, the name of one of King David's sons. In the eleventh company that reached Honolulu in 1844 was a Reverend Eliphalet Whittlesey.

Thorn offers four sets of directions, Michener's adaptation of the Board's actual instructions.

First, the group are to consider themselves as a family, sharing all property in common, relinquishing private goods for the welfare of all. Supplies from the Board, as well as all they might acquire, are to be distributed fairly among the family.

♠ ♠ ♠

Such indeed was the sort of arrangement accepted by members of the first company, but it was one they worked out by themselves. Gathering at the Park Street Church in Boston on Friday, October 15, 1819, they formed their compact and, as faithful Congregationalists, bound themselves "to walk together in a church state, in the faith and order of the Gospel."

It was their close association with each other on the long voyage that demonstrated their need for a more definite agreement among them. Some disputes arose over the dispensation of the supply of wine to be used as medicine, leading to strong feelings and angry words unbefitting such good faithful Christians. To avoid more of such painful differences when working in Owhyhee, the family finally decided to make firm rules governing all their property. It was March 23, 1820, just a week before sighting their destination, that they drew up bylaws declaring that all property would be held in common no matter what its source.

♠ ♠ ♠

Thorn's second injunction is to keep the missionaries on the right religious track and not get mixed up in governmental complications that were not part of their true purpose. He explains it this way: "You are sent not to govern but to convert." Their "divine missions" are to bring the heathen to God and to civilize them.

♠ ♠ ♠

The Board did feel that such a course would be extremely important. They emphasized that their missionaries should "abstain from all interference with local and political interests of the people and to inculcate the duties of justice, forbearance, truth and universal kindness."

To accomplish this, the missionaries must give the people the Bible and the ability to read it and learn God's redeeming ways. The Board directed, "You are to obtain an adequate knowledge of the language of the people; to give them the Bible, with skill to read it; to turn them from their barbarous courses and habits; to introduce and get into extended operation and influence among them, the arts and institutions and usages of civilized life and society." Such concepts naturally meant transforming tropical Owhyhee and its far different culture into a close adaptation of New England thought and life.

♠ ♠ ♠

Thorn then specifies that the missionaries should not engage in trade as their "sole job is to serve the Lord."

♠ ♠ ♠

The Board did realize that herein lay a danger for those practical-minded New Englanders, whose diverse talents might lead them into other fields of endeavor than their ethereal ones. So the Board did designate that "no missionary nor assistant missionary of the Board shall engage in any business transactions or employments yielding pecuniary profit, without first obtaining the consent of his brethen in the missions; and the profits, in all such cases, shall be placed at the disposal of the mission."

♠ ♠ ♠

"Finally," the Reverend Thorn commands them, "you are to lift up the heathen step by step until he stand with you." They were in due time to train the natives to serve as teachers and as preachers.

♠ ♠ ♠

The Board offered even wider and more glorious aims; "Your views are not to be limited to a low, narrow scale; but you are to open your hearts wide and set your marks high. You are to aim at nothing short of covering these islands with fruitful fields, and pleasant dwellings and schools and churches, and of raising up the whole people to an elevated state of Christian civilization." Again the picture of neat, productive, well-organized New England stands before them.

Brave, idealistic concepts came as their concluding precepts. They were told to go "showing unto all men a bright and impressive example of a meek and quiet spirit, and of whatever things are true, honest, just, pure, lovely, and of good report." The final admonition advises, "Do all in your power to make men of every class good, wise and happy." Who could not help saying "Amen" to such a lofty program?

There at Boston, at a grand reception to honor these departing brave souls, a young artist guest offered his services to paint the pictures of the impressive partici-pants of the mission. He was Samuel F.B. Morse, who managed to produce pleasing images of eight of the group. This was 17 years before he invented the telegraph. Would he have included Abner Hale, had such a character been among them? Those he did paint portraits of were the handsome Holmans, the benign Binghams, the refreshing Ruggleses, and the winsome Whitneys.

♠ ♠ ♠

At the time of departure in Michener's story, Jerusha Hale steps forward and presents Reverend Thorn with a packet containing $800, a small inheritance she had received. She explains that, since "the eleven men take no money with them, only these things required on a savage island, it would not be proper for me to take worldly wealth, either." She adds that the money had been meant for her marriage, nobly declaring, "but I have married the work of the Lord."

♠ ♠ ♠

Such renunciation of personal wealth was true to fact. For dedicated Sybil Moseley Bingham did, on her day of departure on the *Thaddeus*, donate that same sum of $800, her worldly fortune, to be used for the work of the Lord in foreign missions. Daniel Chamberlain and his family sacrificed even greater wealth. He had sold his farm at Brookfield, Mass., and turned the proceeds over to the Board, freeing himself and his family to devote their energies to teaching savages the art of farming and the rewards of hard work.

Thus these courageous characters left behind their families and friends, honestly believing they might never see them again, and yet eagerly setting forth on their noble mission. As Hiram Bingham wrote later, "Though leaving my friends, home and country, as I supposed for ever, and trying as was the parting scene, I regarded that day as one of the happiest of my life." He and the others were off on their hopeful adventure with the spirit of the Lord in their hearts.

Most of them did get to return to their "beloved country." Only Asa Thurston and Samuel Whitney would never feast their eyes again upon the familiar sod of New England. Chiefly for health reasons, the others left Hawaii—first the Holmans, then the Chamberlains, then the Loomises, then the Ruggleses, and finally the Binghams. Lucy Thurston revisited her homeland twice, Mercy Whitney once. These two were the last survivors of that pioneer missionary party.

🐜 🐜 🐜

Abner Hale aboard the *Thetis* "had the distinct premonition that he would never again see America." The author had destined him to suffer a miserable demise for his shortcomings of blind faith and uncompromising rigidity of belief rather than allowing him to offer those trusting people of Hawaii the blessings and practical applications of God's loving kindness.

Vll. Life Aboard a Cruise Ship Then

The brig *Thetis* on which Michener dispatches his band of eager heathen-saviors is a ship frightful to behold. "'Oh, no!' one of the women gasped as she saw the squat and ugly little brig *Thetis*. It looked scarcely large enough for a river boat." Michener concedes it was "almost the smallest two-master that could successfully round Cape Horn...It was 79 feet long, 24 feet wide, and drew only a dozen feet when loaded." Jersuha feels qualms about it sinking with 22 missionaries loading it down with themselves and all their supplies.

❦ ❦ ❦

The cargo vessels of that day were rather miniature affairs, considering the distances they had to traverse and the weather conditions they had to survive with the loads of goods and personnel crammed into them. The brig *Thaddeus*, on which the pioneer company sailed, was but slightly larger—85 feet 5-1/2 inches long, 24 feet 7-1/2 inches wide, 13 feet 2 inches deep, 241 tons.

The *Mayflower* had been a bit longer—90 feet—but lighter—only 180 tons—yet crammed with 102 passengers and a hefty stock of supplies. Its stormy trip took 63 days to cross the Atlantic, 101 day shorter than the two-ocean journey of the *Thaddeus*, which carried 23 passengers and a crew of 20. It beat the waves for 164 days to make Hawaii.

The *Thames*, on which the second company sailed to Hawaii, was pleasantly larger for those 22 members, as that brig boasted a span of 101 feet 8 inches, a breadth of 28 feet, a depth of 14 feet, and weight of 350 tons. It made the 18,000-mile trip in 158 days.

The sad scenes attending the departure of the *Thaddeus*, taking away these dear ones heading for an unknown fate, were much as Michener depicts them. The Reverend Samuel Worcester, representing the Board, offered a prayer and then led all present in lending their tearful voices to the tune and meaningful lines of "Blessed Be the Tie That Binds Our Hearts in Christian Love." It was for all a heartbreaking separation. But the break-away must come, and away the missionary party were carried by barge to the already heavily loaded ship in the harbor.

If the brig looked too much on the small side as viewed from the wharf, the scene below decks was enough to frighten any young newlywed with a look into one of the ship's midget "staterooms." Michener describes one as merely "a cubic built for dwarfs…exactly 5 feet 10 inches long by 5 feet 1 inch wide…no windows and no possible ventilation." Those passengers on the *Thaddeus* never forgot that packed-in feeling of four newly married couples being squeezed into 2-foot-wide bunks, lower and upper, in a 6-square-foot unventilated closet. What supreme faith and subservience to their determination it took to reconcile and adapt themselves to such conditions.

♣ ♣ ♣

Poor, lovely, but susceptible Jerusha Hale, in Michener's tale of the missionaries' oceanic trials, is confined to her meager berth for most of the first four months, while her holy husband is beneficently blessed with such a steady stomach that, "although he constantly looked as if he were about to vomit, he ate ravenously and never did." He had to be up and about the Lord's service, sabotaging the sailors' hardy spirits and devil-may-care attitudes, as Captain Janders considered his persistent efforts to convert members of his crew.

Feeling so hale and hearty, ambitious Abner displays an overbearing lack of understanding of Jerusha's condition. Though she lies "pale and exhausted," he forces her to submit to nauseating food and suffer through his Sunday services until the utter force of her illness sends her to the rail, only to fall to her knees and foul the deck with her vomit. Through much of the perilous voyage, the Reverend Hale makes himself an obnoxious, self-righteous monster serving an unfeeling and demanding God.

♠ ♠ ♠

Those aboard the *Thaddeus* likewise suffered in such miserably cramped quarters, bad enough under normal conditions, but to all the discomfort of their squeezed-in state were added the horrors of seasickness—not for just a short time but for the worst part of two months. About four weeks after setting out, Lucia Holman sadly records that "sorrow and despondency were depicted on every countenance, while scarcely a look of love or complacency were discernible one towards the other." Their divine foundations had crumbled somewhat under the pressure of bodily afflictions. Even the stalwart-in-faith Hiram Bingham, suffering badly from gall bladder discomfort and consequent negligence of nourishment during that awful stretch of time, could not muster any active interest in worship and brotherly love.

♠ ♠ ♠

The *Thetis* sails east to the jutting coast of Africa to pass by Cape Verde. Captain Janders arouses expectations of going ashore at Brava. Brava? Wouldn't it be Dakar? Brava is in Somaliland on the opposite east coast.

They cross the equator and then sight "a tall ship with many sails," to Jerusha, "the most beautiful thing I have ever seen." Alas, those who go in the longboat to visit her return in deep disgust and hatred. For that was a slave ship with all its horrors of human degradation.

♣ ♣ ♣

The missionaries on the *Thames* did experience the "horrors" of meeting a Portuguese slave ship. Its "first impressions of beauty" also delighted the viewers, but their feelings turned into revolting thoughts. Charles Stewart stood on deck, looking, wondering, and then shrinking from visions of such cruelties as he knew must exist in the hold of such a vessel. He writhed mentally over such "human misery" and "degradation," boiled in wrath, and called for "the righteousness of God" for "the prosecution of the slave trade...the retribution of a just avenger...on those who make the heavens to echo with moanings of the bereaved, and the earth rich with the tears and blood of the enslaved."

♣ ♣ ♣

The little *Thetis* has to give up on its first heroic attempt to round the cape into the Pacific, but, fortified by the advice of a whaler captain, Janders manages to make it. Michener offers terrifically dramatic scenes of turmoil, with crashing waves, dangerous rocks threatening calamity, and intensely unbeatable obstructions. With ardent prayers and God's help, the *Thetis* victoriously squeezes through the Straits of Magellan.

♣ ♣ ♣

That was not the route of the *Thaddeus*. It sailed down
and around the Straits of Le Maire. The ship's struggles to
gain its Pacific objective are described by Lucia Holman.
On January 26, 1820, she writes: "At 7 this morning we
made the Island of Staten Island on our left—just entering
the Straits of Le Maire. This we deemed the most critical
period of our voyage. The wind having turned against us,
we were driven off and on for 12 hours, in no small danger
of being dashed against the rocks, which border the sur-
rounding islands."

Divine Providence also intervened here and brought
them safely through. Yet the worst was not over. Eleven
days later she added in her diary: "Off the Straits of Magellan,
west of Tierra del Fuego. Last night the winds began to
blow and the seas to roll, as we had never before witnessed;
so that the two conflicting powers seemed to agitate the
ocean to its very foundations. Our vessel labored excessively,
the seas constantly breaking over, threatened every moment
to overpower her. I think I never so much realized the weakness of man, and the power of the Almighty. After all, it is
said we have had an uncommon favorable time in turning
the Cape, such as few experience."

All gave fervent thanks to the Lord that the worst of
their trials was over.

The Unholy Novel

On the long voyage, Abner loses no time getting after
captain and crew to convert them to his own high level

vision of God's will. One moral failing of Captain Janders is his reading of "profane books"—novels. For that, Abner "waged relentless campaign" against the captain, feeling it a stinging affront that he should display such condemned books and even read them "ostentatiously immediately after each Sabbath sermon." Abner warns him he must "learn to call such books abominations."

❧ ❧ ❧

Such was the strict religious attitude of those days toward books that were not "edifying." Sarah, wife of David Lyman, missionary at Hilo, Hawaii, recalls that in her girlhood she "clandestinally" read such books borrowed from another family, because "our parents were opposed to novels." Her son Henry in turn remembers that, in his early youth in Hilo, he discovered in their home "a romance by Miss Jane Porter...but inasmuch as it was a fictitious story, it was placed upon the list of proscribed works." After Henry had become greatly interested in the tale, the book disappeared because "such reading was not profitable for younger boys."

This censorship of juvenile reading pleasures and learning the ways of the world was a precursor of modern-day attempts to remove from school libraries books that certain over-sensitive persons deem objectionable for young readers.

Could those restrained missionaries ever have imagined the license of thought and expression in the 20th century novel, supposedly depicting the life and struggles of one of their number, they surely would have thrown up their hands in horror, feeling that all hell was breaking loose.

Such a book should by all means be hurled into flames—or thrown overboard into the sea, as Captain Janders finally did with his unrighteous novels. This served as his offering for Abner's success in inducing God to get the *Thetis* and its precious cargo of sanctimonious souls past the raging storms that had seemed so impossible to combat.

A Banana A Day

To Abner, a bunch of bananas given him represents a blessing "by the direct will of God." This is food from heaven that can not be ignored. He not only proceeds gradually to devour them himself but, with total disregard for the physical antipathy of his "dear companion" Jerusha to such forceful feeding, he crams some every day into her mouth despite her anguished pleas and mounting nausea.

❧ ❧ ❧

In 1831, when the ship *Averick* with the fifth company of missionaries aboard stopped to repair a broken mast and pick up fresh supplies at Rio de Janeiro, bananas appeared in the stock of food. David Lyman and his wife Sarah "could not [then] abide bananas," according to the later account by their son Henry in his lively story of their missionary days in Hilo, "Hawaiian Yesterdays."

Realizing that such items of nourishment would be prevalent in Hawaii, David hung a bunch of bananas in the Lymans' bunkroom. Each morning he managed to make way with one, so that, by the time they reached Cape Horn, he had learned to enjoy the flavor of this unfamiliar fruit.

Even Sarah recorded in her diary a month later, "Ate our last banana to-day brought from Rio." Evidently she too had learned without coercion to partake of such food.

♠ ♠ ♠

Michener's agonizing banana episode finally does end favorably. Jerusha at last is freed from her daily banana ordeal and enjoys the soul-satisfying delight of tossing the last of the offending fruit into the ocean. With fresh vigor and self-determination, she asserts her independence. "You bullied me," she accuses Abner, "through your sin of overzealousness." He was not to get away with such sheer domination over her another time, she decides. "I am as good a judge of God's will as you," she points out, "and God never intended a sick woman to eat so hatefully."

Had Abner lived a century later in a lighter mood, he might have tried to cheer up poor fruit-frustrated Jerusha with a bit of gay song, such as:

Yes, we must eat bananas;
We must eat bananas I say.
For the good Lord has sent them;
We must not resent them
Or gaze on them with any dismay.
So don't be so suspicious
That they aren't quite delicious

And sent with God's best wishes
For us to enjoy them each day.

That Irresistible "Sanctified Joy"

On the long journey, as Jerusha's condition improves, she is learning how to handle the demon that Abner sometimes makes of himself. To her, God appears in a more kindly, generous light than Abner's concept of the Divine Being. He looks up at "a distant, living, full-bodied, vengeful yet forgiving God."

When Abner sternly denies the Bible to the poor sailor whose efforts aloft courageously save the *Thetis*, Jerusha daringly gives the man her own Bible. To Abner's frightened dismay, she is rewarding a backslider. Then she refutes Abner's objections by declaring that "the idea of God has no meaning for me unless at such times He is willing to meet an evil old man with love." Jerusha becomes in the novel the better side of the missionary spirit, helping Abner to see the right when his overzealous demands lead him too far astray from the path of better understanding.

Abner stands dumbfounded at her mention of the idea of God, "but, before he could continue his charges, Jerusha, with her liquid brown curls dancing beside her ears, kissed him once more, and they fell into the narrow bunk." Thus Abner finds himself irresistibly succumbing to Jerusha's "intoxicating" influence and the "sanctified joy" of his pleasure with her. Soon after, Jerusha is "in the first happy flush of pregnancy."

♣ ♣ ♣

In the confines of the *Thaddeus* such a scene never occurred. No self-respecting missionary, had he ever dared to read such a novel as this and managed to get this far past other evidences of evil worldliness, could have restrained from gasping in despair at the utter shamelessness of depicting this offensive conduct in print. Even more inconceivable is it that any of those purely pious missionary wives, filled with "overpowering religious fervor," could ever have behaved in such an unseemly way.

But the law of nature must have prevailed even in the cramped sleeping arrangements aboard the diminutive *Thaddeus*. For, among the six newlywed couples that arrived in Owhyhee aboard this ship, four wives delivered children before nine months after their landing. Maria Loomis was the first to become "in a delicate condition," bringing the first missionary child to young Elisha and Maria within four months after their arrival. The other births came from 6-1/2 to 8 months after.

The *Thaddeus* arrived in Kailua-Kona on April 4 and in Honolulu, April 19, 1820. Levi Loomis was born July 24. Marie Kapule Whitney did not appear until October 18, Sophia Moseley Bingham on November 9, and Sarah Trumbull Kaamualii Ruggles on December 22.

The other two of the newly married men might have seemed the most likely candidates for fatherhood. Dr. Thomas Holman, unlike the hastily married quartet, qualified by reason of his longer friendship with Lucia

Ruggles. During the voyage, the others accused the Holmans "of practicing and justifying the most sickening familiarity in the cabin and on deck." Later they were charged with "holding hands, kissing each other, and openly demonstrating affection in public, thus flagrantly and sinfully corrupting the morals of missionary children and heathen," according to Dr. Francis J. Halford in his revealing accounts of the "Nine Doctors and God."

The Holmans' daughter, Lucia Kamamalu, did not make her appearance until March 2, 1821, nearly a year after their arrival, while the Thurstons' first child, Persis Goodale, waited until the following September 28 to join the missionary family. Athletic, virile Asa, being the eldest of the newly married, must have developed greater restraint, perhaps accentuated by his "born again" Christian reform from what he so deeply considered his ill-spent youth. He and Lucy had truly been, as she expressed it, "crucified to the world…their hearts fixed on the glory of God in the salvation of the heathen."

VIII. WELCOME TO HAWAII

The *Thetis* reaches the Lahaina port amid a wanton offering of feminine flesh. To offer such an active, eager market in damsel delights as Michener pictures at that period is somewhat surprising, as the whaling industry, with its demanding, sexually-deprived sailors, was just getting going so early in the decade.

🏵 🏵 🏵

Quite different from such a scene were the arrivals of the first two mission ships. As the *Thaddeus*, and then the *Thames* three years later, passed the shores of Kohala along the north coast of Hawaii, natives in canoes scurried out to greet these strangers. Their appearance and lack of dress differed so decidedly from that of the strait-laced Yankees that the missionaries' abiding impression of these wild natives could be only one of savage, uncivilized creatures scarcely recognizable as human beings. Hiram Bingham on the *Thaddeus* spontaneously dubbed them as destitute, degraded, barbaric, naked savages. He and his comrades shuddered at this dreadful spectacle of depraved humanity, wondering whether they could ever succeed in shattering "this deep pagan gloom."

Charles Stewart on the *Thames* later experienced similar scenes and the same direful forebodings. To him, these excited natives appeared as "wretched creatures" with "wild expressions"—an exhibition of "uncivilized character" that made them seem to be "half-man and half-beast," perhaps the missing link "connecting man with brute." A ship's officer, agreeing that these savages could be only "brutes in the shape of men," assured his truly human passengers that they could never stay to live among such terrible specimens of mankind.

Unfortunately, such dismal views of the people persisted and were repeatedly voiced by later missionary arrivals. To these loyal New Englanders, their homeland was the pride of civilization and their precise religious beliefs the sole criterion for judging others.

Those Hefty Hawaiians

To Abner Hale at Lahaina, the impressive scene was—after he had beheld a naked woman for the first time—the picturesque arrival of Kanakoa's father and mother, "two of the most gigantic human beings Abner had so far seen." Malama, all 320 pounds of her, loomed 6 feet 4 inches tall, with forearms "larger than the bodies of many men," and "her gigantic middle...more like the trunk of some forest titan than of a human being."

♣ ♣ ♣

When Bingham first received royalty as the *Thaddeus* made a brief stop at Kawaihae, he admitted these chiefs appeared "ponderous," but felt their weight has been exaggerated, deciding in his precise way that it must average 266 pounds. Kuakini, the high chief who later received the missionary party at Kailua, did strike Bingham as being not only "tall, portly" but "gigantic." Later viewers of Kuakini's immensity claimed he bulged to over 400 pounds and had to turn sideways to wedge his bulky frame through the doorway of the present Mokuaikaua Church.

Laura Judd reports the Binghams' view of Liholiho's five wives: "They are all of immense proportions, weighing three or four hundred pounds each." Then Laura comments, "I have been silly enough, in my younger days, to regret being so large; I am certainly in the right place now, where beauty is estimated strictly by pounds avoirdupois."

High Rank Above All

Malama ranks as "the highest chief in the islands," as her son Keoki declares, and adds, "When my father wants to ask her a question of state, he has to crawl into the room on his hands and knees. So do I."

🐜 🐜 🐜

Fictitious as this may seem, so it was even with the great Kamehameha, who married his niece, Keopuolani, a top-ranking chief. As Russell Apple, a professional historian delving into Hawaiian lore, explains the mighty king's situation, this queen's "status was like that of a goddess. Keopuolani was so sacred, and outranked her husband so much that Kamehameha the Great crawled into her sacred presence." The king first had to make an appointment to see her. "Before he entered her house, he took off his only clothing, his loin cloth. He had enough mana (divine power) to associate with her, but for him to wear anything in her presence was an insult."

"By Keopuolani, Kamehameha the Great had two sacred sons and one sacred daughter. They all outranked their father…(so that Kamehameha) was supposed to prostrate himself—faced down—when his sacred son Liholiho approached him,…but instead…he lay face up. Liholiho used to run to him and sit on his great father's great chest."

Display Of Royal Standards

Impressive indeed is the arrival of the royal couple, Kelolo and Malama, coming from the shore in "a large canoe, with vassals…bearing yellow-feathered staffs."

These were the *kahili* always carried by attendants when any *alii* (chief) appeared in public. Bingham describes the arrival at the *Thaddeus* at Kawaihae of two queens in their double canoe with "the nodding kahilis or plumed rods of the nobility."

Small *kahili* were useful in chasing the flies off the chief, and such likely was the origin of these standards. The great ceremonial *kahili*, carried on poles 20 or more feet high, were designed with a wide variety of native bird feathers. They were carefully stored in calabashes until needed for display again. Today's reproductions aptly use dyed turkey feathers.

Taking On A Big Load

A "considerable commotion" aboard the *Thetis* sends the missionaries scurrying "to witness an extraordinary performance. The huge bulk of Malama is being hoisted aboard with great care and concern in "a rugged canvass sling that was customarily slipped under the bellies of horses and cows, hoisting them in this fashion onto the deck of this ship."

This was the method for loading cattle from Kailua and other island ports but not until the next decade. Excessively weighty as they were, the heavy chiefs could still get around and board ships naturally.

♠ ♠ ♠

Once deposited safely on deck, Malama breaks into tears at the distressing sight of the skinny missionary wives. She takes up little Amanda Whipple and hugs her to her expansive bosom as if she were a child.

❧ ❧ ❧

Lucia Holman received similar queenly consideration when one of the huge queens who came aboard the *Thaddeus* examined her hair and lack of bulk. As Lucia tells it, "She got me into her lap, and felt me from head to foot and said I must cow-cow [kaukau] and be nooe-nooe [nui nui], i.e., I must eat more and grow larger. She admired my hair very much, and wished me to take out my combs, and let her see how long it was. She then wanted to see how I rolled it up."

Enjoyable Lahaina A Better Place

By landing at Lahaina, Michener's missionaries found a much more welcome sight than the pioneer company ever did at Kailua—or even Honolulu. Here Abner sees his first coconut tree and "orderly fields reaching away to the hills, so that all Lahaina looked like one vast, rich flowering garden." Keoki points out the dark green breadfruit trees and the kou trees providing wonderful shade.

❧ ❧ ❧

Charles Stewart, landing there a year after this fictional arrival, considered the place at first "far more beautiful than any place we have yet seen on the islands," as he admired the "luxuriant groves" of coconut as well as of breadfruit and kou, "an ornamental tree resembling...a large and flourishing, full, round-topped apple tree." He relished comparing the landscape with the attractive features of his fondly remembered New England. And the thoughts of his "four weeks' residence on the dreary plain of Honolulu," made Lahaina appear "like the delights of Eden." He found also the banana, tapa and sugar cane abundant. But then, fond memories of his dear New England began to intrude and he started deploring the lack of "uniformity or neatness" in the arrangement with so much growing "in the wilderness of nature."

Far from such an Eden-like scene confronted the pioneer missionaries on their arrival at arid Kailua on April 4, 1820. The place was so forbiddingly barren that none of them would have really chosen to remain there. The scene presented none of the rich greenness and flowering beauty of today. Just rough, dark, hardened lava rock formed its surface. Bingham saw Kailua as "a dry and sterile spot…ornamented with cocoanut and Kou trees."

Lucia Holman shrank from the rough living there— on the bare rock of lava, which left "not a spot…large enough for a garden, but what is covered with Lava and cinders." When she later got away to Lahaina, she reacted delightedly at the sight of all the vegetation there, claiming she had not seen anything in the way of such greenery before on the islands.

IX. QUEENS AND THE NEW DRESS FASHION

The irrepressible Malama on board the *Thetis* puts on a big show illustrating the basic differences of dress between her and her new-found lady friends from

America. She arrives in native costume, "her bundles of tapa making her seem even larger than she was." Overheated by her exertions in getting loaded on deck, Malama, like a giant top, unwinds the great roll of tapa encompassing her mighty bulk, thus ridding herself of all that covered her fleshy form. This strip performance causes one of the missionary ladies to faint at the horror of so much exposed nudity. Keoki hurriedly advises Malama to cover herself, "for Americans hate the sight of the human body."

♣ ♣ ♣

A similar scene did occur aboard the *Thaddeus* at Kawaihae when two dowager queens came aboard. They appeared, attired by request, in the native dress, the *pa'u*, "which," Lucy Thurston noted, "consisted of ten thicknesses of the bark cloth [tapa] three or four yards long, and one yard wide, wrapped several times round the middle, and confined by tucking it in on one side. The two queens had loose dresses over these.

"Trammeled with clothes and seated on chairs, the queens were out of their element. They divested themselves of their outer dresses. Then the one stretched herself at full length upon a bench, and the other sat down upon the deck. Mattresses were then brought for them to recline in their own ways."

Lucy later describes the process of getting dressed up in the voluminous *pa'u*. Kamamalu, Liholiho's favorite queen, seeking a special attire for a grand royal feast, asked to borrow one of Lucy's gowns. But "it was among the impossibles for her to assume it." So the queen had to wear a *pa'u,* "enveloped round the middle with 70 thicknesses. To array herself in this unwieldy attire, the long cloth was spread out on the ground, when, beginning at one end, she laid her body across it, and rolled herself over and over till she had rolled the whole around her. Two attendants followed her, one bearing up the end of the cumbrous robe of state, and the other waving over her head an elegant noddly flybrush of beautiful plumes [a *kahili*], its long handle completely covered with tortoiseshell rings of various colors."

♠ ♠ ♠

Malama soon catches on that new fashions are coming in style. She must "dress as the new women do." With that decision, she imperiously orders Jerusha and Amanda to make an American-style dress for her. Which they do—a "tent-like" one. "Now," she declares joyously, "I am a Christian woman!"

♠ ♠ ♠

The true story of such a happening involves those same two queens whom we left lounging on mattresses aboard the *Thaddeus* at Kawaihae. These two plump widows of Kamehameha, Kalakua and Namahana, sailed with the missionary party from Kawaihae to Kailua. "Kalakua," Bingham relates, "shrewdly aiming to see what the white women could do for her temporal benefit, asked them to make a gown for her in fashion like their own. Putting her off until the Sabbath was over…they cheerfully plied scissors and needle the next day, and soon fitted out the rude giantress with a white cambric dress."

Such generosity of dressmaking by the kind-hearted missionary wives eventually boomeranged. All these generous efforts to win the approval and support of the chiefs were made willingly at first. The missionaries worked hard to try to satisfy their royal hosts by supplying their ever-increasing demands. Thus they won favor and gained some early successes.

But the going was hard on them, as they struggled to establish their own cherished ideas of civilization. After the limitations on cleanliness during that six months' voyage, they had all their garments to get washed and, of course, ironed. Native help proved to be useless for such careful treatment of fragile clothes. So Bingham and his group, after getting settled in Honolulu, carried their piles of clothing out to what the women called a "heathen brook," and, rejoicing "in the Divine goodness, which daily supplies the needful strength for these new scenes and untried labors," they suffered on "while the tropical sun was withering their physical powers, and literally blistering their arms."

Besides all this demanding enterprise, Mrs. Bingham had just managed to get a school started when Hopu popped in from Kailua with "a piece of fine shirting" and a request for her to "make for his Hawaiian majesty five ruffled shirts with plaited bosoms, to be sent back to him at Kailua by the vessel returning in a few days."

"Such demands from the king, his wives, and other chiefs, male and female" kept acoming, and Bingham regrets that "in our destitution of not a few of the daily comforts once enjoyed, and an anxious desire to give full satisfaction, required some sacrifices, and caused, during the first years, some expenditure of health and strength on the part of those who were willing thus to toil."

Consider what these too-accommodating wives had to put up with in their attempts to win favor by their assiduous plying of scissors and needle to create becoming fashions for some haughty chiefess. Bingham pictures the poor missionary wife taking the new dress that had been requested and having to wait uncomfortably for an hour or so while her ladyship was merrily playing cards. "Then, on trial, hear her laconic and supercilious remarks, 'pilikia—hemo—hana hou' (too tight—off with it—do it over); then see her resume her cards, leaving the lady, tired and grieved, but patient; and when successful, to be called on again and again for more."

It was four or five years later, Bingham relates, before this business of tailoring and dressmaking to win royal recognition finally reached its climax. One "woman of rank" came to a missionary wife asking as usual to have a dress made for her. Then she soon came back for a second, again for a third, and then for a fourth. The first three were made "promptly and gratuitously," but by this time the woman showed this was to be an endless series of fresh expectations. The missionary wife decided it was time to call quits.

Having previously taught the woman's girls to sew, she suggested they make a dress for her. But, no, that would not do. They were too lazy and would take too long, the woman declared.

But the missionary wife had had enough. She told the woman, "I am here alone in feeble health. I sew clothes for myself and my family. I have not a company of servants about me to come and go at my bidding. Much of my cooking and other work I must do myself. I have a number of scholars to teach each day. I have made for you three dresses, and taught your girls to sew. I appeal to you to say whether I ought now to do the fourth." Bingham reports, "She felt the rebuke and waived the request."

Neither did Malama release any flow of gratitude for all the women's labors in dressmaking. For her world was one "in which all but she were servants." Lucia Holman was impressed by the same queenly attitude in Kailua. "Her Royal Highness, one of the Queens,…appeared astonished to see" her and Lucy Thurston busily arranging their goods deposited from the ship. When Hopu explained to her that in America the women were "always doing something, [and] that they were seldom idle,…she expressed surprise and pitied us, saying we must not trouble ourselves about anything, but must have servants."

Thus the missionaries found it was no easy task to keep toiling and trying to please those in high position and power. But they persevered.

♣ ♣ ♣

Before letting her massive body be swung down from the ship to her waiting canoe, Malama takes off her expansive new robe. Once ashore, being carried along in her canoe-like conveyance on the shoulders of ten huge men, she again has the precious dress slipped over her head to display herself in all her new finery. And the women squeal, "Maikai! Maikai!" (Good! Good!)

♣ ♣ ♣

"Maikai" was one of the first words Lucy Thurston had a chance to hear and remember as the ship was approaching Kailua. Looking out, she sees "a canoe of chattering natives with animated countenances; they approached and gave me a banana. In return I gave them a biscuit. 'Wahine maikai,' (good woman) was the reply."

The dress that Lucy and her companions had put together for Kalakua, the dowager queen with "limbs of giant mould," was received at Kailua with wild acclaims too "by hundreds with a shout" as she stepped out in her "newly-made white dress...with a lace cap, having on wreath of roses, and a lace handkerchief, in the corner of which was a most elegant sprig of various colors...presents we had brought her from some American friends."

♣ ♣ ♣

At the king's royal request, Dr. Thomas Holman and Lucia remained at Kailua with the Thurstons, who were elected as the ones to establish the first mission there.

Part Two
PROBLEMS IN PARADISE

X. Climate, Clothes, Diet And Disease

Michener condemns the missionaries for their stubborn adherence to their precious New England life style in their refusal to adjust themselves to their new tropical environment, neglecting the experience of the people who had survived salubriously under sunny skies. "All the accumulated wisdom of the islanders was ignored by the mission families," he declares. "Perspiring in unbelievably heavy clothing, eschewing the healthful foods that surround them, they stubbornly toiled and grew faint and lost their health and died."

♣ ♣ ♣

Health was naturally a primary problem the missionaries had to face—both their own and that of the people they had come to civilize and save. Much is true in what Michener offers as their faults. But they did manage to make out and not die off so stupidly as the novelist implies. The folly of fashions and the proper selections of food were their chief stumbling blocks, as they kept on going overdressed, overworked, and sometimes overfed with the wrong kinds of food.

The Dictates Of Dress

Two weeks after Abner, with all his memorized book instructions, had successfully manipulated the birth of their son Micah, Jerusha "was teaching her classes again, a slim, radiant missionary woman sweating in a heavy woolen dress."

♣ ♣ ♣

The missionaries' clothing problems stemmed from their imbued customs. Their way of dress was "civilized;" the natives' absence of attire was "heathenish." These men of God and New England could not bear to think of adopting the natives' relish for real comfort and their carefree attitudes towards leaving exposed such broad areas of their physique.

Sereno Bishop recalls "the good old times" when a "bevy of ladies led by a royal dame, all fresh from their sea-bath, and in nature's array" invaded the Bishop sitting room and, not until then, proceeded to cover their bodies with the clothes they had carried with them from the beach, as they gayly chatted with their hosts.

Really shocking! But missionaries in heathen lands had to put up with offenses like that on occasion. No sea-bath sporting for them. Their only acceptable process of bodily cleanliness was a good old bathtub dousing, or at least a good fresh water rub-down. The problem was the scarcity of aqua pura at Kailua. So, as Lucia Holman sums up the situation: "The natives use fresh water only to drink; they bathe in the sea."

But not so, the missionaries. To these Northerners, now dwelling in "the latitudes most pampered by Providence," with no such experience in the icy waters off the "stern and rock-bound coast, "enjoyment of their aquatic advantages in the warm ocean was restrained by their religious-imposed modesty. They would have been shocked by the thought of frolicking in the inviting waters of the Pacific as Halford pictures Hopu and Kanui at Kailua, leaving the missionaries to their labors and going off for "a sunrise swim with Kona youths, maidens, matrons, and men, sporting like so many seals and as unhampered by dry goods."

Although Hiram Bingham did admire the Hawaiians' "powers of diving and swimming, and the dexterity and ease with which they manage themselves, their surf boards and canoes," he was pleased to note: "The adoption of our costume greatly diminishes their practice of swimming and sporting in the surf, for it is less convenient to wear in water than the native girdle." This decline of custom "as civilization advances," he felt, kept the natives from wasting time in idle sports, and he was satisfied that this was not being caused by "oppressive enactments against it" by the missionaries but by "the increase in modesty, industry or religion."

At church the natives did try to show some modesty. Abner decreed they "must be dressed as proper Christians." To his bleak satisfaction, he was pleased to see the native women managed to hide even "the offensive nakedness of the wrists," though he noted that their costumes displayed "the essence of practicality and ugliness."

Hiram Bingham encountered similar problems. In his determined efforts to "save their souls" by correcting "their uncouth and disgusting manners" and improving "their modes of dress and living," he found some amusement and sometimes pain "to witness the efforts of some of the noble women...attempting to put off their heathen habits, and assume a more civilized air," resulting in "grotesque and ridiculous combinations" of dress. But, by 1827, Bingham was proud to proclaim, "You see everyone decently dressed in our own style." Thus American fashions in due time prevailed over native comfort, ease and indifference.

Dr. Halford cites an amusing missionary reaction to the native lack of modesty. Uninitiated Laura Judd "stood aghast, in doubt whether to retire, or stand my ground like a brave woman, and was ready to cry with annoyance and vexation" because, on entering the Binghams' kitchen to make breakfast her first morning there, she came upon "a tall native man, clad much in the style of John the Baptist in the wilderness." She confessed, "I am verdant enough to be shocked, and shall use all my influence to increase the sale and use of American cottons."

In turn, Dr. Halford became aghast at the ignorance her conclusion showed. For, he points out, she did not know such a policy of swathing the body in cloth would "increase no end also the incidence of respiratory afflictions due to wetting and evaporation which rendered the enforced use of cotton clothing so much poison to a people whose nakedness had been for centuries a perfect prophylactic."

The poor missionaries suffered their own personal problems of keeping themselves fittingly clothed. Their own source of apparel was from the scrimpy pile of clothing grabbed at a first-come-first-supplied basis at the annual general meeting in Honolulu. Sent out by the Board in Boston, these misfit garments were merely the "unsalable residue of various slop shops," and, even so, "not always sufficiently numerous to supply the needs of all," according to the memories of Henry Lyman. He tells of William Richards arriving so late he found he was literally left "out in the cold." This was indeed "a dreadful disappointment, for his only pair of black trousers was in the last stage of disintegration; and in what other color could he appear before the Lord as an honored and God-fearing ecclesiastic?"

His loyal wife came to his rescue in his predicament by fashioning for him from a treasured black satin skirt "a suit of staid and sombre hue...of a genuinely evangelical pattern." Then the missionaries' opponents seized upon this finery to malign these religious gentlemen, claiming they were dressing up in "nothing less expensive than the costliest silks and satins."

Sereno Bishop well remembered the "assortment of ready made slops" worked off on "the poor missionaries" by their fiscal agent, Levi Chamberlain. He conscientiously admitted that "much of the clothing did not appear to be adapted to the human form." The missionaries in Bishop's day (1830's) were "simply clothed in garments...nearly all cut and sewed by their wives, and could not have been very stylish. They very commonly appeared in the old-fashioned short jacket. I never saw a frock-coat in Kailua, only the claw-hammer,"—Abner Hale style.

A covering for the head was another missionary fashion dictate. The sensible native custom was to go bareheaded except sometimes for protection from the burning sun. Oh, but that was not the way in New England. People wore hats, and "those poke bonneted Priscillas" never went to church with their heads not adorned by a bonnet. So it must be in Hawaii, the missionaries decreed.

Lucy Thurston had at first seen "not one woman in the nation, and but one man, with a covering on her head. The first native woman who was seen with a bonnet in church was the bride of Thomas Hopu in August, 1822."

She had been well trained by Lucy, who then went on to train other native women to make and wear "bonnets of oat straw and sugar cane...line them with white kapa...thin like cambric, and trim them with kapa ribbon, colored in figures." That pleased Lucy. "They looked very neatly," she approved.

Even 15 years after the Thurstons' arrival, Lucy's counterpart in Hilo, Sarah Joiner Lyman, kept struggling to overcome the native female aversion to wearing a bonnet. She persuaded all her large class to braid new bonnets, but before long some had abandoned them entirely. She tried again with bonnets that really made them look "quite respectable." But she soon found "they laid aside their bonnets altogether and wore their hats only occasionally."

Undeterred, she talked each woman separately into the bonnet-wearing custom until none dared come with uncovered head. Another heathen custom she could not tolerate was the native way of "ornamenting the head and neck with wreaths of flowers and beads. To her, such decorations were a sad waste of time, as they did not last. She made them tabu in her school and used her influence with church members "to put them down."

The chiefs more naturally took to show-off and fashions and to copying foreign examples. Governor John Adams (as he preferred to be known as, instead of by his native name Kuakini) heartily approved the bonnet style and "made a law that no woman should enter his yard without a bonnet..." Later he extended this law to the church, much to the missionaries' satisfaction.

Not so favorable to the bonnet brigade were Chester Lyman's observations. On his tour of Hawaii, he attended Sunday church service at Waiohinu, August 23, 1846. "The people," he wrote, "were most decently dressed & some of the women had on hideous apologies for bonnets. There is nothing so out of all manner of taste as putting bonnets on the heads of these females. In their native headdress of full curling hair bound by a cincture of ribbon or a wreath of flowers they look free & in good taste, but an old fashioned rumpled, dirty cast-off bonnet stuck crown up hat fashion on the top of the head transforms them into hags, resembling the poorest dressed negro wenches." Lyman preferred "a headgear...unlike that of foreigners, but adapted to their complexion & general appearance."

He complained also of the "absurd imitation of English or American fashions" to compress the generous native form into the tight dress. "The simple loose dress, which has been worn all over the islands, is easy, cool & very becoming. But put these buxom savages...into corsets & they appear like a monkey in small clothes in agony & ill at ease until the offensive encasement is laid aside."

How much dress, fashion, and custom meant to the missionaries' concept of proper appearance before God!

How different today! Among week-day visitors to the historic missionary church in Kailua-Kona, appear scantily clad lasses unabashedly entering the sacred building—enough to make one wonder what those staid founders must be muttering, if they may be looking down from the heartily-sought haven of their heavenly home. They must indeed be shocked by the uncovered heads, bare limbs and peekaboo breasts that to them marked the sinful female.

Difficulties Of Diet

Choice of food is a matter of background, habit, individual taste and availability. Those were the diet problems the missionaries had to deal with. They failed to free themselves entirely from their preformed preferences, adapting themselves according to their individual inclinations.

Idealistically bent, the missionaries did come to Hawaii with false dreams of recreating on the islands by their diligence and know-how familiar sources of agriculture to provide them with their home-style table fare. The Board held the same concept—that their cohorts on those foreign shores were "to aim at nothing short of covering those islands with fruitful fields."

Albertine Loomis depicts such erroneous anticipation in the mind of the missionary farmer, Daniel Chamberlain, who, she conceives, "had envisioned vast stretches of Hawaiian lowland furrowed and planted, acres of ripe wheat,…maize bursting with ears, flour and meal and cow's milk for every heathen child." And also, of course, for the long-deprived, hungry missionary families themselves. Such desires did not entertain the minds of the Hawaiians. They were quite content with their fish and poi and native fruits and vegetables.

Dr. Halford faults the missionaries for their avoidance of a better balanced diet. "Meals were too heavy, too frequent," he asserts, "lacking elements required by the climate, and containing many not needed or positively injurious." Yet he has to admit that newcomers to Hawaii still show the same lack of acceptability to native fare at the pretentious luaus offered tourists—feasts "replete with sufficient assimilable calories to make a mouse fight a wildcat." But, spurning such unaccustomed tastes, these diners end up at a drugstore for a dessert of ice cream, claiming, "I'm full, but I just don't feel satisfied."

Considering the condition of their own far-shipped American supplies, why weren't the missionaries just thankful for the presently available fresh food? Whatever food allotment the Board shipped to them arrived in miserable condition after six months' storage in a ship's hold. Their much-appreciated yearly allowance of a barrel of flour for each family came "commonly mouldy, and full of large white worms," as Sereno Bishop well remembered. Even the rice from China reached them "very weevly."

Bishop watched his father and Asa Thurston divide a flour barrel, "solidly caked, mouldy for two inches in, and thoroughly wormy. It was all eaten except for the mouldy exterior." (Perhaps they eliminated the worms too.) After the hardened flour had been pulverized by pounding, his mother carefully sifted it and then would add "an equal bulk of boiled sweet potato thoroughly rubbed in, so as seldom to betray its presence," making it "fairly light and far better than no bread." As Lucy Thurston's bread was much darker, Sereno surmised she worked poi into hers.

What seemed silly to Dr. Halford was that these people should pay to have flour shipped to them when "no end of taro could be had for the asking." But that taste did not satisfy these new arrivals brought up on bake goods.

Laura Judd and "a missionary sister" sat one morning distressed at the prospect of trying to satisfy their "craving appetite" with sweet potatoes and spoiled imported salt beef. Such limited and repetitious food selections naturally seemed dreary and inadequate to their developed fancies and robust appetites. Frustrated, Laura shelled out four shillings and the servant brought back "a pound and a half of fresh beef for 50 cents! We broiled it, and with our hot cake made a delicious meal." They just could not help relishing such a bit of luxurious dining.

The Thurstons and Bishops did make progress in developing native food sources. Up the mountain, they had "flourishing orange trees and grape vines, and were well supplied with taro, sweet potatoes, bananas and sugar cane." Besides, they had fresh pork, chickens, turkey and fish, and milk from "a good flock of goats...and the kids were delicious eating." So, Sereno concludes, "I think we always had enough food to eat." All he missed were Irish potatoes and fresh beef, the latter being unavailable because the wild cattle were up "on Mauna Kea, on the other side of the island."

The only periods of real deprivation occurred during returning periods of drought and famine, when the people had to subsist on whatever foods could be found. Bishop remembered the "severe experience in the twenties," when the mission families in Kailua were saved by "a blessed God-send when rain came, and a plentiful crop of wild mustard sprang up, furnishing abundance of boiled greens."

Thus the missionaries managed to adapt themselves according to their inclinations, interests, and circumstances. But, at first, decided change of diet and some deprivations did add to their health problems. Albertine Loomis concludes, "So they suffered from lack of their customary food. It was not strange, then, that they were all prey to disease, that letters spoke of sisters 'confined to their couches,' of 'symptoms of impaired constitution,' of 'extreme prostration and debility'...that Samuel Ruggles grew so thin, sallow, nervous and dyspeptic that the whole company worried about him; or that the second and third Bingham children were born with too little vitality to stay alive."

One favorite Hawaiian food they spurned was poi, giving it a very unworthy bad reputation. It is quite different from ice cream, being too often put down as tasting like library paste. Bingham wrote that it is eaten, "cold and unseasoned" and "would serve well for bookbinder's work." Sarah Lyman had no taste for poi, which her husband had learned to eat. He told her that, if she were to eat out a few times where she could get nothing else, she'd learn to eat it.

Author H. Allen Smith (not a missionary) refused to try poi because he felt others ate some just to be able to say they did. His wife did, made a face, and called its taste "some distance removed from delectable." But for nutrition it is unexcelled, a perfect baby food. Dr. Halford praised it as having "few if any equals in the present-day world of dietetics" for its "digestibility, nutriment, and balance."

Lucia Holman, the missionary with probably the most finical tastes and disdain for things Hawaiian, voiced her objections to the native sustenance. She complained that "hogs, fowls, fish, tarro and [sweet] potatoes" were "all of an inferior quality," ill-flavored and lacking sweetness, though she did enjoy banana and melon. To her, breadfruit had just "an insipid taste," quite contrary to Charles Stewart's appraisal, "one of the finest of our vegetables." Lucia's general reaction to island fare was that "the fruits and vegetables that these islands produce taste heathenish."

The Struggle For Survival

With health problems the missionaries did suffer, as their sad reports home revealed. Hiram Bingham assessed the causes to be "the climate of perpetual summer," over-energetic activities in their eager effort to succeed in their enterprise, and "the privations and unaccustomed modes of living and [the] hardships."

Bradford Smith points out such troubles were due to their "stubborn inability to alter their own habits to fit the climate." Mrs. Stewart's "health...beyond recovery" was blamed partly on the "debilitating climate." Dr. Abraham Blatchley, the second missionary physician, left after three and a half years. Though he declared his "constitution much impaired by the climate," he was worn out from trying to serve the physical needs of the missionaries scattered about on different islands. A later physician, Dr. James Smith, came to realize that Hawaii has "the most healthy climate in the world and did the people take proper care of themselves and properly obey the laws of our physical nature there would be but little sickness among them."

The missionaries just worked too hard in heavy clothing and with disregard for temperature. That was their New England legacy of toil. Instead of adapting to the leisurely life style of the tropics, they labored on, grew weary, and succumbed to weakness and illness. "Much ill-health," Dr. Halford asserts, "was due to wrapping up from toenails to topknot in clothing a tenth of which would have been too much for this uniformly mild climate." He agrees with Dr. Blatchley's worried concern over "the multitudinous chores of the Mission women" and disdains their wasting too many hours "ironing frilled shirt fronts and petticoats, alternately soiling and washing innumerable duds and dishes." That they kept on toiling thus without native help he blames on the "lack of understanding between the highly individualistic and prideful native and the custom ridden Puritan woman."

Dr. Thomas Holman, pioneer missionary physician, was the first to give up and leave, after only a year and a half in the islands. Back at Bridgeport, Conn., he lasted only four more years, dying of "lung fever" caused, the family claimed, by "overwork and worry" in Hawaii. At age 32, he was the youngest of the first seven missionary men to die.

Daniel Chamberlain, oldest member of the company, went back after three years, partly because he felt the climate endangering his health, and lived to be 78. Elisha Loomis, youngest member, after seven years of service as printer and teacher, returned because of ill health and died at age 36.

Hiram Bingham found his health situation getting critical after seven years. Suffering effects of overwork and "chronic hepatitis, apparently preying on my vitals," he decided the only way to prolong his doubtful life span would be to get away from "the perpetual summer of our dusty Honolulu" and his cares and strenuous labors there. The Binghams spent two months in a mountainside cottage five miles from Kailua in Kona, regaining fresh energy and spirits in the cooler atmosphere. They left Hawaii after 21 years because of his wife's failing health but hopefully expecting to return. In this he was disappointed, for she suffered along for eight years more to die at age 55. He carried on to 80.

Samuel Ruggles, whose early health problems had so worried his comrades, "pulled through to live 14 busy years in Hawaii…His vigor returned sufficiently to beget six lively children, with enough left over to take the whole family back to America…and to carry on," Dr. Halford notes, to age 76. His companion, Samuel Whitney, remained on the islands to serve there faithfully for 25 years until his death at age 52.

The devoted and determined Thurstons at Kailua were the long-suffering, faithful hangers-on. Lucy served as a striking example of health problems missionaries might suffer and as a paragon of indomitable courage to carry on and survive.

A tubercular condition brought on by over-exertion at the time of her mother's death recurred in Hawaii after the birth of her daughter Lucy. She recovered again; then three years later "the hard struggles of pioneer life, its efforts and its privations again prostrated me with pulmonary complaints. Nature triumphed and I was again free.

"Scarcely a year had elapsed, when we were visited by storms of fierce winds and deluging rains, uncommonly long and severe…home was damp, cold, and bleak…Disease took fast hold of my frame, and became obstinate." She felt she "should die of consumption. Four years passed before I was restored to my vigor."

Then, on the way from Kailua to Honolulu in the brig's cabin, which reminded her of "the Black Hole of Calcutta," Lucy had to endure childbirth with the aid of only her husband and Artemas Bishop. Later, it took her three months to recover from her "nearly fatal mistake of taking strychnine instead of quinine." She made two return trips to Boston and back, thus enduring in her lifetime about two and a half years spent in the confines of those small sailing ships.

Tumor of the breast brought on another experience of Job's lot. Lucy sat for an hour and a half in a chair while the doctor cut out her entire breast, the glands beneath her arm, and sewed up and bandaged the foot-long bloody wound. After it was all finally over, the doctor took her hand and admiringly declared, "There is not one in a thousand who would have borne it as you have done."

Such was the superior strength and faith in the Lord of one of the first missionaries to Hawaii. The frailest of her family, who fully expected she was sacrificing herself to early death "in that heathen land," Lucy kept active until her death at age 81, the last of the missionaries who remained in Hawaii. She lived a few months longer than the life span of her hardy husband.

Asa served most of his 41 working years in Hawaii at the Kailua mission, retiring to Honolulu only when strokes of paralysis forced him to give in. He died there seven years later at the age of 80, the same age as his companion Bingham. Lucy and Mercy Whitney, who

lived to be 77, were the only pioneer missionary representatives left to join in the mission's 50th anniversary
celebration in 1870.

The record over the ensuing years of missionary activity in Hawaii is one of generally long life. Of the 169 total
(84 men and 85 women), only 24 succumbed before their
40th year. Thirteen attained the ripe age of 90 or over,
five men and eight women, and two of the women reached
101 and 105 respectively. In their 80's were 38 more, while
another 41 were still active after 70, making a total of 92
who surpassed their allotted three score years and ten.

Chief causes of demise were tuberculosis and "dysen-
tery," which might cover other intestinal diseases, including typhoid and food poisoning. For women, child-bear-
ing was, in those times and conditions, a risky affair that
sometimes caused death.

The Fading Hawaiians

Michener's more liberal-minded Dr. Whipple brings
up the concern about the rapidly diminishing native population. Having witnessed entire villages vanish when the
measles epidemic struck, he foresees that the population
originally estimated by Cook at perhaps 400,000 will be
cut down to a mere 30,000 in the next 30 years. Then
"this dreadful plague" strikes again, "destroying an already
doomed population." Keoki perishes along with his people,
accusing Abner with "Your god brings only pestilence."

✿ ✿ ✿

The missionaries did strive valiantly to stem this tide of destruction of the race, having early realized its causes and terrifying effects. William Ellis, in his report on "Hawaii" in his "Polynesian Researches" series, considers the 400,000 estimate "somewhat above the actual," even though he had seen numerous evidences of formerly populated areas abandoned. His own estimate in 1823 came to not more than 150,000.

Ellis explains what caused this extreme decline: "The rapid depopulation...within the last 50 years, is to be attributed to the frequent and desolating wars;...the ravages of pestilence, brought in...by foreign vessels;...the awful prevalence of infanticide; and the melancholy increase in depravity, and destructive consequences of vice."

Confirming Ellis's judgment, Bingham cites a report late in 1826 by John Young of conditions he had observed during his 49 years of residence: "I have known thousands of defenceless human beings cruelly massacred in their exterminating wars. I have seen multitudes...offered in sacrifice to their idol gods...and this large island [Hawaii], one filled with inhabitants, dwindle down to its present few numbers through wars and disease." Ellis three years earlier figured the population on Hawaii then to be about 85,000.

Titus Coan traces the decline in population from "long before the arrival of the missionaries," when "a pestilence like a plague swept off multitudes." He attributes this disaster to vile foreign diseases, too rapid a change in national habits, and the ruinous wiles of certain foreign visitors. Such radical changes, he explains, as "in dress, in food, in dwellings, and in occupation of life, often bring on consumption, fevers, and other diseases which almost decimate a community. Natives that once lived as nude as the brutes, and were yet hardy, because adapted to their surroundings, often succumb to new habits of life."

By 1836 "the missionaries saw," Bingham says, in issuing their doleful report, "that unless Christianity could arrest the causes of desolation, the ruin of the nation was certain." So they determined "to labor for this people as 'pulling them out of the fire,'" spreading throughout the isles the religion Young had supported and to them "the only sovereign antidote to this dreadful contagion."

In that same year, Artemas Bishop cited figures of the depopulation on Hawaii from 80,000 in 1821 to but 50,000 in 1827, and one tenth more from 1832 to 1836. This roused fears that the Hawaiian would be extinct. Historian Kuykendall supports this, stating that about 1840 the decline was so evident that extinction was "freely predicted."

Even the natives tended to feel they were doomed. Chester Lyman in 1846 noted that David Malo, Hawaiian historian, "seems to be deeply impressed with the conviction that the nation is destined to run out &

give place to the whites. This conviction is growing in the minds of the more intelligent natives, & cannot escape the observation of any reflecting person." With the population of the islands down to 85,000 in 1850, an editor in Honolulu predicted only 100 Hawaiians surviving by 1930.

Dreadful epidemics were killing off thousands of the Hawaiians so susceptible to these foreign diseases. Titus Coan reported, "In 1848 a fearful epidemic of measles carried off 10,000 of our people, a tenth of the whole population. Five years later the smallpox took 3,000 more...The natives were strangers to these diseases; physicians were few...The natives had no remedies for these burning plagues...Tormented with heat and thirst, they plunged by scores and hundreds into the nearest water...and the eruption being suppressed, they died in a few hours.... And now, for many years,...leprosy has been poisoning the blood and lowering the vitality of thousands."

"Thus," Coan concludes, "the decrease of the Hawaiians goes on slowly, surely, irresistibly...before the unrelenting march of civilization"—one imposed on them by invaders from beyond the seas.

These dire forecasts of total extinction fortunately did not come to pass. Though the Hawaiian population declined by 1872 to a mere 44,000, in 1930, instead of a sad remnant of only 100, the census found 23,000 full Hawaiians and 28,000 part Hawaiians.

Precisely how many really "pure" Hawaiians existed then or do exist now is largely a matter of good guessing. For over a hundred years, part Hawaiians, ignorant of their past racial mixture, still considered them selves really "pure" of blood. A survey in 1931-32 showed only 1700. This kept varying under different survey methods. The 1960 census listed 11,194. A 1971 report found "well under 1000." Another report four years previous showed 130,000 with some Hawaiian blood, 18,000 more than in 1960. A State Health Department survey in 1972 brought in a figure of 150,000. With such gains in numbers, a new estimate suggests that by the year 2000 Hawaiians will again fill their isles with 300,000, hopefully hale and hearty.

What has caused such a reversal of trends? Devastating diseases eliminated the weak strains. Out-marrying with other races produces a new race with strength and beauty, even though it is not the pure Polynesian stock of the times before Cook's advent.

The late Samuel Crowningburg-Amalu, columnist for the *Honolulu Advertiser*, pondered this situation in a column on "The Last Hawaiian" some years ago. He concluded that the Hawaiian "close to survive but he had to pay a tremendous cost for that survival. He had to give up every thing he was, lose everything he had. He had to make himself over again and, in the process, become something new. And there, right there, lies the Hawaiian tragedy. In order to survive, the Hawaiian became the spiritual dependent of western culture and thereby lost his own soul."

The missionaries had come to save souls. The grace they bestowed upon the people was their own interpretation and belief. The early acceptance of the strict religion they imported has scattered among a variety of irreconcilable faiths. Today the Protestants rate third place behind the Catholic and the Oriental forces.

XI. Erase The Heathen Devils

Abner's abiding view of the Hawaiians was that they were vile. That stemmed from his first view of the naked savages, when female flesh was unrestrainedly revealed and offered. "'Almighty God!' he prayed. 'Help us to bring light to these cruel hearts. Give us strength to strike down each heathen idol.'"

     🐾 🐾 🐾

As we have seen, the missionaries on arrival were also seized by impressions of the depravity of those poor souls they had come to save. The Reverend Sheldon Dibble, who arrived in Hawaii with the fourth company a decade after the first ones, still could not refrain from continuing to classify the people as "low, naked, filthy, vile and sensual; covered with every abomination and stained with blood…down into the deepest mire and heathen pollution." The Binghams and the Thurstons repeatedly made the same accusations against those "heathen savages."

That meant that God's servants had a great work to do, and they certainly meant to do it. So they set about reforming these errant ones who where heir to and had acquired such evil faults. One quite evident failing was the natives' indolence. They just lacked that New England enthusiasm for good hard work. Lucy Thurston looked down upon the people as being "destitute of motive to activity or enterprise."

It took a missionary physician, Dr. Alonzo Chapin with the fifth company that came in 1832, to point out the health advantages of the natives' easy way of life. "They walk with a slow step, rest long and often when tired, and placing no value on time, they do everything leisurely and to suit their convenience." Such a life style fitted the climate and saved them from many afflictions endured by their new hard-laboring foreign friends.

To make matters worse, according to the missionary minds, those unambitious natives wasted their time in play games, sports, gambling and dancing—all so useless. Bingham complained that "Gambling was shown to involve the wasting of that time…needed for moral and mental culture…and for honest industrial pursuits." The one required time of rest lay in the strict observance of the Sabbath, dear to the hearts of the missionaries. They renounced all activity for that day except the worship of God.

So the missionaries felt compelled to drive the people to more hearty endeavors, but from which they must cease entirely on the holy day of the week. Yet worse than such problems were two imported evils which they had to combat—tobacco and hard liquors.

The Vice Of Smoking

Abner, "the little white cockroach," as Malama's handmaidens gayly called him, sees all the evils weakening her people and her nation and dramatically points them out to her. A house burned to the ground represents the terrible effects of smoking. The death of four people in that fire is a lesson that Malama should "outlaw the use of tobacco." Later, Abner is investigating another "home that burned because the owner smoked tobacco." As this time the offender survived the fire, Abner just "admonished him for his sin."

♠ ♠ ♠

As the missionaries did find just such situations, they used their influence to outlaw the foul weed to prevent its tragic consequences. Quite innocently, the Hawaiian eagerly accepted both the good and the bad that the white introduced, especially if it afforded some element of pleasure. They then availed themselves of it without restraint or consideration of its evil consequences, tending to carry on their new-found pleasures to excess.

The Lymans in Hilo observed that the native use of tobacco was much more extreme than that of the foreigners who had introduced it. They noted that the natives "swallow down the smoke and are consequently frequently intoxicated, some times falling into the fire and some times into the water."

Lorenzo Lyons found later, "One great reason why the natives are so wedded to tobacco is because of the intoxicating effect. Several houses have been burned with parents and children in them because the adults were stupefied with smoking." He had previously reported, "Some individuals had smoked to intoxication, and fell into the fire, no one being near to help. They were burned to death."

Another native evil was the addiction of small children. Lyons on one occasion "found six smokers among very little children. They promised to give it up." His wife Betsey was pleased to write, "Some whole schools of children have given up smoking tobacco." Lorenzo saw also the prevalence of family indulgence in smoking: "After a meal sometimes," he noted, "the big wooden pipe is taken out and passed around, and everybody in the family takes puff, even to the four year old child."

The Thurstons found smoking an objectionable feature of native life, even aboard the ship taking them back to Kailua. In the cabin Lucy suffered this situation: "It is impossible to tell how often the pipe came along, passed from hand to hand, from lip to lip, and the room became perfumed with all that is odorous in tobacco smoke, rising and issuing from their mouths as from a chimney." No fire-hazard restrictions or non-smoking sections in those days.

Because of the intoxication and consequent fatalities, Lyons established anti-smoking societies and ordered, "No church member is allowed to plant this pernicious weed." He added, "If he plants it he is disciplined—if he repent not he is cut off."

But this church policy ran into such difficulties that Lyons admitted in a report to the Board that he expected "much trouble on the subject of tobacco." The trouble was that the king and "most of the chiefs" favored tobacco, commanded their subjects to plant it, and enforced such orders by condemning those who might refuse, perhaps taking away their lands so that they would be "stripped of everything." But Lyons held this hope: "Some fearing God more than man will not comply with this command."

When reprimanded by Samuel Whitney for her continuous smoking, the queen of Kauai wanted to know, "is it forbidden in the Scriptures?" "No," Whitney admitted, while declaring, "but you make it a sin by using it to excess."

This produced favorable results. "She bowed to his displeasure and responded, 'Here is my pipe. I will smoke no more.'" Bingham adds to this account, "Others soon followed her example, and many were reclaimed from the useless, costly, filthy habit."

The Lymans in Hilo seemed able to get favorable results with less coercion. Mrs. Lyman had the women sign her "tobacco roll," agreeing to give up the pipe. In 1836, she happily recorded, "The tobacco reformation is gaining ground…Those who are disposed to leave off smoking are requested to call and leave their pipes and tobacco with us, and when a sufficient quantity is collected, we are to make a bonfire." But she had to admit, "It is no less hard for them to leave off than for the drunkard to forsake his cup."

So it was that, as the authors of "Puritans in the South Seas" saw it, the "fulminations against pipe-smokers were almost as bitter as those against drunkards." They cite the situation in Lahaina, where missionaries Mrs. William Richards and Miss Maria Ogden "led a campaign against smoking, and induced the wives of smokers to prevail upon their husbands to give up the 'filthy habit,' regarded as 'one of the fires that kindles the thirst for spiritous liquors.' Within a few days, 2,500 men had been persuaded to bring their beloved pipes to the mission house for confiscation. Some smoked until they reached the missionary's threshold, then took one long puff and surrendered the source of one of their greatest pleasures."

Titus Coan in Hilo was one of the severest opponents of the weed. Refusing to "tolerate devotees of tobacco," he drove them out of his church rather than permit such waywardness.

Today tobacco is still a problem although there is progress to diminish its use. Though not proclaimed a "sin," it is still a "vile weed" to many, offensive in its use and dangerous to health. And people still perish in fires caused by careless smoking.

Demon Rum

Another evil Abner points out to Malama is the dreadful influence of imported liquors—"whiskey" in Abner's term, though rum was probably the most popular strong drink. Such a harm also should be outlawed. But, in making the new laws, Kelolo points out that sudden stopping of the sale of alcohol would be disastrous to merchants already well supplied. Jerusha's suggestion of stopping the import of new supplies brings out the restrictions imposed by French warships. Kelolo reminds them that they "made us promise to drink lots of: their alcohol each year" and even "said we had to make Hawaiians drink their alcohol, too." Just the same, Malama includes in her announced laws, "From today no more alcohol may be sold to Hawaiians."

& & &

The narcotic juice of the awa root was the common drink of the Polynesians. It is still enjoyed and used for ceremonial occasions in Fiji and other Pacific Islands. These people also fermented drinks from sugar cane, sweet potatoes or ti root.

The work of the devil in teaching the joy-loving Hawaiians how to manufacture distilled liquors is recorded by Archibald Campbell, who spent 13 months in Hawaii, three of them living with King Kamehameha in 1809. Later the king gave him 60 acres of land with 15 families of servants. Though he had three houses, because of his crippled condition he preferred to live with William Stevenson, a convict escaped from New South Wales, "but [who] was, notwithstanding, an industrious man, and conducted himself in general with great propriety."

This Stevenson introduced the method of distilling a strong alcoholic drink from ti root. The eager natives quickly figured out how to make their own simple stills from iron pots they got from American ships. The liquor got its name, okolehau (iron bottom), from those iron pots. It became the leading national drink, winning a prize at the Paris Exposition of 1898.

Stevenson so reveled in his product that the king felt "obliged to deprive him of his still." So Stevenson reformed and took "an oath, not to taste spirits except at the new year, at which time he indulged to great excess." Noting the popular consumption of the liquor, Campbell feared "the consequences will be more pernicious...Both whites and natives are unfortunately too much addicted to it. Almost every one of the chiefs has his own still."

Stewart laid the blame on Stevenson and his promotion of distilleries for causing drunkenness to become "one of the most common vices," with "general inebriation, when men, women, and children are...under all the excitement of liquor."

At the king's house, Campbell had full opportunity to observe what went on in the household. Though at one time the king was "strongly addicted to the use of ardent spirits,...finding the evil consequences of the practice, he had resolution enough to abandon it." Campbell adds, "I never saw him pass the bounds of strictest temperance." Kuykendall records that Kamehameha "is said to have proclaimed a stringent prohibitory law." But his son Liholiho failed to follow his father's fine example, "and during his brief reign drunkenness became distressingly common throughout the whole kingdom."

Queen Kaahumanu also took to her pleasures instead of joining her royal spouse in abstinence. She played safe while the king was around, but "she generally availed herself of his absence...to indulge her propensity for liquor, and seldom stopped short of intoxication." She sometimes amused herself getting two companions drunk, only to put herself in the same condition.

Such was the moral situation when the missionaries arrived. When the first company reached Honolulu, they found the high chief Boki "through the influence of strong drink...unfit for business." They right away declared, "This is a stubborn foe with which we shall be obliged to contend."

In their tour of Hawaii in 1823, Thurston, Bishop and Ellis found abundant cause to lament the general inebriation of people in the villages. Besides this deplorable situation among the populace, Liholiho was setting a dismaying example for his people and a disgusting one to the missionaries. Stewart, on his arrival at Honolulu, finds the king still drunk in a spree of several days. Again he sees the king so intoxicated he could barely keep his seat on his horse.

Later, at Lahaina, Stewart is shocked by the scene of the king and his court lying about, sleeping off their drunkenness, near empty cases of brandy, gin and rum.

After the death of the king's mother, Keopuolani, Stewart witnessed scenes of "drunkenness, riot, and every species of debauchery." But Liholiho then renounced his liquor until some conniving foreigners fooled him with a bottle of cherry brandy and got him into another "dreadful revel."

Appalled by such intemperance, the missionaries carefully set their course to control it not only by laws but by wise principles. Bingham admits that "no state has been known to abolish the traffic in ardent spirits."

After converting some of the leading chiefs, the missionaries got them to call on their faithful followers to promote general temperance "by sound argument, safe example, reasonable pledges of abstinence, and a vigorous support of government…Every communicant in the various churches was taught to discountenance and avoid the manufacture, sale and use of ardent spirits."

Stewart cites the case of the high chief Kalanimoku, previously "notorious for his…intemperance in drinking," which caused him to commit "the most wanton outrages." But he had reformed under missionary influence and "entirely abandoned the habit." Governor Hoapili cut down on the drinking of rum on Maui, Molokai and Lanai. In general, the control of over-indulgence soon appeared promising.

Artemas Bishop, on another walking tour of Hawaii just two years after he had found it "a most common thing to see whole villages given up to intemperance," happily reported, "Drunkenness is suppressed by law. In my whole tour I saw but one man intoxicated." On Kauai, Peter Gulick, four years later, was able to announce, "The natives are prohibited from all commerce in ardent spirits, and from using it, except as a medicine." Consequently, he "had not seen an intoxicated native, nor heard of one."

But Honolulu was never such a favorable hope for temperance because of the strong foreign counter attempts. Bingham wrote of 260 foreigners there, "most of whom claimed the privilege either of making, vending, or consuming the deleterious beverage." These "yawning, pestiferous rum holes" preyed upon the poor sailor boys, Bingham asserted, causing them to part with their "money, clothes, reputation, and peace, at a dear rate."

The free-living Boki, unlike the converted Christian chiefs, showed little regard for the ideals of temperance. Bingham complained, "He set up a store and tavern in Honolulu, and encouraged the manufacture, sale, and use of intoxicating liquors." He also leased a sugar mill to a company, who converted it into a distillery for making liquor from the sugar cane. But Kaahumanu, seeing his product being "converted into poison," had potatoes planted in place of the sugar cane.

This flagrant misuse of the liquids that enliven was a new problem to these missionaries brought up in the friendly atmosphere of New England society. At the Thurston home in Fitchburg, the visiting minister enjoyed his glass of "the best flip." Ursula Emerson, daughter of the energetic Rev. Gad Newell at Nelson, N. H., amazed her Hawaiian-born children with her tale of having to go as a young girl to fetch a quart of rum for the exchange minister. Her son Oliver Emerson offers another unbelievable story of so much liquor being consumed at a church dedication "that a special detail of police was ordered to preserve decorum and suppress any undue hilarity."

Such early familiarity with occasional overdoses of joy juice paid off for Ursula. The church and Sunday school at Waialua were to give a concert. The conductor of the concert lay over the wall in the graveyard, too drunk to lead. Though he protested his inability to get up, Ursula demanded he come home with her. After he finally managed to stagger along to her house, she made him down a "dose of hot ginger tea," which rendered him "sober as a judge." Thus revived, he made the concert such a complete success that it also insured the Sunday school superintendent's winning public office in the coming election. It had been the superintendent's political opponent who had craftily made the conductor drunk.

After Boki, the situation in Honolulu improved somewhat when Kuakini took over the post as governor of Oahu. But his success in promoting restrictions was weakened by the bad conduct and influence of the young Kamehameha III, who licensed grog shops again. The growing temperance movement in the 1830's and the strong support of high chiefs brought a law against drunkenness in 1835 and then two liquor laws in 1838. These came to naught the next year when Captain Laplace imposed a treaty that included a clause against the prohibition of wines and brandies.

What to do about the excess use of liquor is a never-ending problem. Everything looked bright again to Laura Judd in 1843, when she wrote, "Temperance laws are now triumphant." But, by 1851, she reported heavy controversaries waged by newspapers and their readers over native distilleries, making of wine, and reducing the duty on liquor. They "argued that high duties increased smuggling, that cheap liquor diminished drunkenness, and that a moderate use of wine was Scriptural, and conducive to benevolence and long life." Such positions "brought down an avalanche of statistics to prove a contrary opinion."

This heated debate stirred opposing ire for months, "till the subject was threadbare." And still the problem continues.

That Uncontrollable Urge

"The Lord...and all civilized nations agree..." declares Abner, but to specify the evil in words leaves him too ashamed to speak of this terrible sin of mankind. Screwing up his courage, he manages to blurt out, "There shall be no adultery."

Then he becomes confounded by Kelolo's revelation that "in Hawaii we have 23 different kinds of adultery. " The solution for phrasing the new law was "Thou shalt not sleep mischievously."

♠ ♠ ♠

It is true. That is how the missionaries had to word that important commandment. The Hawaiians had no such word as "adultery" in their language and no classification of "illegitimate" children. Sex was a natural, free part of life and "mischievous sleeping" was an expected part of it, lending added fun with no reproach in general. Before the time of Captain Cook and his infected men, no physical afflictions resulted from such promiscuity.

The missionaries were only too well aware of the disastrous effects of these communicable diseases and doubly alarmed by the moral degradation they ascribed to such freedom. They continually referred to the natives as "licentious," "lecherous," "depraved," engaging in "debauchery."

Titus Coan became deeply alarmed at the moral situation. "They are amorous...and the seductions of vile men from foreign lands, endanger the morality, the piety, and the life of this infant race." Sex was a force impossible to restrain, especially under the liberties of the past and the foreign impositions of privilege at that time.

"In the old times," wrote Mark Twain in 1873, "to speak plainly, there was absolutely no bar to the commerce of the sexes. To refuse the solicitations of a stranger was regarded as a contemptible thing for a girl or a woman to do; but the missionaries have so bitterly fought this thing that they have succeeded at least in driving it out of sight—and now it exists only in reality and not in name."

XII. The Horrible Hula

Though Abner Hale had never witnessed a hula performance, he knew full well it was just another vicious evil and so "had often railed against this dance." Thus that afternoon "when he heard...the muffled, haunting throb of a pagan drum," he knew that meant natives were staging "the long-forbidden hula." He sets right out to hunt down those "lascivious revelers and punish them." But he finds them not—only "sweet-faced men and women practicing hymns."

Frustrated, he sets out in search of evil doers again that evening. Then it is that he comes upon the setting for those dismaying Keoki-Noelani nuptials. But what arrests his attention first is the appearance of six women, "naked to the waist and with red flowers in their hair, necklaces of polished black nuts about their shoulders and anklets of shark's teeth which clicked as they began an ancient hula."

Abner did not rush up to forbid it. In fact, he became rather fascinated as "the swaying skirts made of ti leaves moved in the faltering shadows. As he watched, "he noticed how solemn and graceful the dance was, for the women seemed to be disembodied spirits, undulating in response to night winds: a movement would start in their heads, work its way along their supple arms, and pass to their hips in one unbroken symmetry of motion. Abner had to concede that such was not the terrible exhibition of evil forces he had been led to expect. His idea had been "that naked men and women..." But he did not have time to complete the thought.

Michener's other reference to the hula comes from Dr. Whipple after he has spent two weeks in Tahiti. One of his profound observations is that the "most spectacular" of the changes that occurred as the Tahitian seafarers settled in Hawaii was "the transformation of the bold, angular and oftentimes lascivious Tahitian hula into the languorous, poetic dance of Hawaii."

♣ ♣ ♣

Missionaries' irritation with and objection to the hula started from the very beginning of their life in Hawaii. At Kailua, determinedly striving to win Liholiho's consent for their stay in the islands, they were eagerly expecting another audience with the king and chiefs, when "two native dancers appeared,...and a band of rude musicians, singing, and drumming on calabashes." Then the dancers started "this heathen hula," which held the attention of the king, chiefs, and multitudes for what seemed an unduly long time for the impatient missionaries.

A year later Bingham complained that too many of the people, "with greater enthusiasm [than for schools and public lectures] were wasting their time in learning, practicing, or witnessing the hula, or heathen song and dance." But, like Abner Hale, he observed and recorded the elements of the hula with more interest than respect. He described in detail the hula dancers' decorations, their arrangement, movements, the musicians' instruments, and the singing. Charles Stewart and William Ellis also paid careful attention to such dance demonstrations and carefully described similar details.

Such "detailed and spirited descriptions of native ways" prompted those at the Hawaiian Mission Children's Society to point out that students of Hawaiian culture today "have reason to be grateful" for these well documented details. They also refer to Bingham's "only mild disapproval" of a hula performance before the king and his refraining from breaking up the dancing, "as Abner Hale would have done." Bingham, they explain, "only asked quietly that the hula not be held on Sunday—and Governor Boki just as politely refused the request." They approve that Stewart's description of the hula performance was written "with zest and vividness. Though he rejoices," they add, "that such customs 'will soon be lost forever in the light of civilization and Christianity now rapidly dawning,' he makes it clear that the missionaries were fascinated spectators at such affairs and that they did not try to censor the celebration."

Just the same, Bingham's inclinations were such that he plainly wanted to eliminate such interference with his plans for "civilizing" these heathen who wasted so much time and energy in such worthless and debasing activities. To him the continuous hula practice was noisy, distracting, and disturbing. The musicians' instruments were "unharmonious." Worst of all, he believed, "their old hulas were designed to promote lasciviousness, ...interwoven too with their superstitions, and made subservient to the honor of their gods." Their purpose was just to serve the pride and pleasure of the king.

Bingham's wrath boiled up more fiercely when he witnessed "the mirthful, giddy dance of the ungodly pleasure-seeking throng [brought] into the midst of death and mourning." This occurred during the loss of Kalanimoku's favorite wife, Likelike, in 1821. Bingham tried to convince the king that the dance was "connected with idolatry and licentiousness, and wholly incompatible with Christianity," but the king "affirmed that it was play and not idol worship." The missionaries at that stage were experiencing difficulties in impressing the chiefs with the virtues of their religion.

Arriving at Honolulu in 1823 after his long voyage, Stewart was just in time to witness most of the elaborate celebration marking the annual feast to commemorate the death of Kamehameha. He delighted in the grand displays, pronouncing the royal pageant emphatically "splendid," though partly apologizing with the hope that his readers would "not altogether condemn the epithet." Nor could he allow himself to enjoy fully the "companies of singing and dancing girls and men," though he faithfully described the scene and sounds. But these "enthusiastic adulations" of the highest chiefs, he must add, "fell on the heart with a saddening power; for we had been compelled already from our own observation, as well as from the communication of others, necessarily to associate with them exhibitions of unrivalled licentiousness, and abominations which must for ever remain untold."

Improvements in the chiefs' religious attitudes did come to encourage Stewart and relieve his dismay over the hula. He rejoiced later at Lahaina over "another triumph" that demonstrated that the chiefs were gaining respect "for the new system over former habits of folly and dissipation." At prayer time he had found "an immense crowd...assembled" to watch 18 female dancers, accompanied by seven male musicians. But the whole court and many natives broke away and put an end to the dance to join him and give great attention "to the religious exercises that followed."

In the postscript to his book he could finally exult that, "In the region of every Missionary establishment, the songs, and dances, and games, and dissipation, once so universal, had entirely ceased." Unhappily, the "brethren were constantly urging the prohibition of most practices previously enjoyed by the natives," as Louis B. Wright and Mary Isabel Fry explain in their "Puritans In The South Seas:" "Their sports and games found no favor in missionary eyes. The hula was of course a snare of Satan."

That the hula could on occasion appear not so bad to a missionary, William Ellis reveals in his reference to the dancing he observed outside Keopuolani's house in Lahaina. The dancers' "movements were slow, and, though not always graceful, exhibited nothing offensive to modest propriety," he admits. At Kailua, he witnessed hulas performed for Governor Kuakini, described them in appreciative detail, and after one of them he preached, taking as his text the Bible warning to "turn from these vanities unto the living God."

Thus those early missionaries eagerly observed and recorded the elements of the hula, but at the same time their overbearing religious attitude overrode their sense of full appreciation. As the high chiefs came to accept the rigid religious standards, even to them the long-honored ceremony became the hated and unlawful "lewd and lascivious hula."

This repression did drive the hula into its more suggestive demonstrations where degenerating displays delighted the whoopee-loving whalers at the notorious grog shops. But after the death of that strong Christian character, Kaahumanu, in 1832, the ancient hula again gained royal support during the reigns of the last three Kamehamehas. They revered the ancient traditions and revived the hula, though not without fomenting renewed efforts by the greatly alarmed church gentry.

Heeding the outcries against social indecencies such as the hula, the government in 1851 put on stiff regulation of all public performances. As the hula was still receiving royal sanction, a renewed surge of moralistic oppostion reared up in the later 1 850's. Demands for the suppression of the hula became more vociferous as even some Hawaiians, responding to the missionary call to goodness, came out in protest against what they were led to believe were the evil elements of their culture. Representatives of other newly established churches felt it their duty too to join in condemning this wanton waste of spirit, energy and time.

Aiming to squelch this blot on public morals, a dozen missionaries in 1858 drafted an urgent request two pages long demanding that Kamehameha V "take such legal measures as will effectually suppress this great and increasing evil." The terrible tendencies of the hula they proclaimed were demoralizing multitudes, leading them back to degradation by diverting them "from all industrial and intellectual pursuits," causing them to neglect their fields and gardens, interfering with the schools, and fostering "idleness, dissipation, and licentiousness to produce poverty and distress," thus developing into crime.

Strenuously backing such denunciations of the hula was Henry M. Whitney, editor of *The Advertiser* and son of Samuel Whitney, one of the pioneer missionaries. The editor believed the hula was actively "spreading contagion" and warned that "so infatuated do males and females become under it, that it will be in vain to urge them in industry or to any efforts to raise themselves above brutes."

One of the missionary signers of that hearty denunciation of the hula was the Reverend John S. Emerson. He and his wife Ursula devoted their energies to helping the Hawaiian people, most of their time (26 years) at Waialua and four years at Lahainaluna.

They had seven sons and then one daughter. Their seventh son, Oliver Pomeroy Emerson, served as corresponding secretary of the Hawaiian Evangelical Association during the trying period of the change-over from monarchy to territory of the United States. He recorded his parents' careers as missionaries in "Pioneer Days in Hawaii."

Of a rather different trend was their fourth son, Nathaniel B. Emerson who devoted his talents to researching and preserving the lore of the hula, publishing his learned account in "Unwritten Literature of Hawaii: The Sacred Songs of the Hula." Nathaniel was not one to denounce the hula as essentially immoral. As a sincere scholar seeking truth, he could explain, "The hula was a religious service in which poetry, music, pantomine, and the dance lent themselves, under the form of dramatic art, to the refreshment of men's minds. Its view of life was idyllic, it gave itself to those mythical times when gods and goddesses moved on the earth, and men and women were gods."

Another missionary descendent later expressed regrets at the earlier missionaries' condemnation of Hawaiian culture. Ethel Damon blamed those misguided religious leaders for having failed to look beyond the "crust of barbarism which met their first glance- and thus the old civilization, poisoned by ignorance and neglect and stung to death by ridicule, was vanishing forever." She was the granddaughter of the Reverend Samuel Damon, pastor of Bethel Union Church, Seamen's Chapel, in Honolulu for 42 years and editor and publisher of *The Friend*, a paper critical of such royal policies as the encouragement of the hula.

After Kamehameha V and Lunalilo came King Kalakaua with his hearty revival of Hawaiian tradition and culture, bringing back into life the ancient music and dance as well as creating new hula steps, movements and instruments, including the ukulele, to develop attractive combinations of ancient and modern.

Conservative-minded missionaries still scowled at dancing of any kind as a deviation from high religious principle. Sarah, wife of the Reverend David B. Lyman in Hilo, expressed her disapproval of the report that "several of the children of missionaries are fond of the amusement [of dancing] and engage in it. She voiced her doubt that "you can ever find really devoted christians among dancing christians." Although she had to admit the absence of really any sin in dancing, she felt "it always brings reproach when christians do it."

Such remarks appeared in a letter in 1868. In 1874, when King Kalakaua visited Hilo, she regretted that he was to be entertained with "hulas and meles and other heathen practices." Recollecting that such dancing had been introduced into Hilo when the former King Lunalilo had paid the town a visit, she was pleased to add that, though the natives had indulged in such excess then that they had "three dance houses all of bad reputation," they "have all gone down."

So the hula kept on having its ups and downs and ins and outs. With the overthrow of the monarchy in 1893, puritan elements began to dominate again and look with scorn and loathing at the hula and the "heathen" Hawaiian culture. But the true devotees of the hula kept their faith in and fervor for their beloved art and privately carried on their study and practice of the hula, developing masters of the dance who would spark the renaissance later.

The foreign influence was coming to the fore as new songs began to be staged with English or mock Hawaiian words, Tin Pan Alley ragtime music, and accompanied sometimes by Satan-incited motions. Hawaii and the hula became almost synonymous in the entertainment world and among the lures that beckoned tourists to the enticing Pacific paradise. And again rose the demands that this debasing influence of the notorious hula be stopped and this thorn in Hawaii's reputation be plucked out.

This popularized entertainment that became a universal fad was merely a modernized perversion of the true hula. As such it was roundly condemned by serious supporters of a culture basically Hawaiian as a travesty of the supposedly divine-inspired hula. They regretted seeing Hawaii represented mainly by merry South Sea island fantasy and to have people everywhere consider the hula as an example of "the riotous and passionate ebullitions of Polynesian kings and the amorous posturings of their voluptuaries." But big-time adaptations of the hula and the spirit of Hawaii flourished around the world in song, dance, plays, movies, and island promotion. It ranged from the idly idyllic to the sometimes idiotic.

People were enjoying it, but the true hula had not yet come back into its own production.

It was the "hula greats" who kept studying, practicing and developing the ancient art that finally brought forth adaptations accepted as truly representative of old Hawaiian influence. Its greatest display today is at the Merrie Monarch Festival held each spring in Hilo. Dance troupes from around the islands gather there to compete for honors. The demonstrations are the product of careful preparation of songs, dance steps, costumes and staging. Both men and women groups take part amid tremendous applause from a mighty audience. One night is devoted entirely to the ancient traditional hula, the next to the lighter modern hula. It all is a grand occasion for both artistry and fun—even a "missionary hula" with girls primly clothed in high-collared muumuus swaying prudishly.

The missionaries had had their beliefs and ideals and had fought forcefully for them. But the hula has won its way back as an admired art form and society has come to accept it as such instead of a lure of the devil. In modern views also a little naughty fun is not something to get too provocative over. In today's world people have found other really repulsive factors to protest.

XIII. THE SQUANDERING OF SANDALWOOD

Abner Hale is confounded again. His work requires the promised church must be built, but Kelolo is dodging the pressure for such accomplishment. Another evil is at work. Chief Kelolo's people—2,000 of them, men and women—are being driven high into the mountains to gather loads of the diminishing supply of sandalwood: "the lifeblood of Hawaiian commerce, and the goal of all Americans...the treasure and the curse of Hawaii."

Here was a comparatively useless, free product for which the chiefs could gain the grand goods they coveted. Kelolo is to own the *Thetis* by supplying two well-packed, ship-size pitfuls of sandalwood. The people stagger in with their heavy loads, pack them into the pit, and then on command trudge back for more. Later, Abner meets the weary army of sandalwood salvagers again, to discover they are scrounging for every last remnant—even "saplings and roots grubbed out of the soil."

♠ ♠ ♠

The white men's big ships offered one of the leading lures for ambitious, luxury-loving Hawaiians. In their eagerness to display such fine styles of living, the king and chiefs readily committed themselves to meet the high demands of the crafty Yankee traders. Liholiho, King Kamehameha II, had inherited from his father the sandalwood monopoly but not his parent's sagacity and power. The chiefs pressured him to share this national wealth with them, and then they went on squandering it willy-nilly in succumbing to seductive sales pressures and their greed for fancy riches, Liholiho leading the way.

What new, young, heathen king, eager to display his grandeur, could fail to be dazzled by an offer of the most luxuriant ship of the decade—*Cleopatra's Barge*? Not Liholiho! Without so much as bothering to consider his dwindling resources of the eagerly-sought wood, he casually promised 8,000 piculs (each 133-1/3 pounds) of his precious commodity—a price of about $80,000.

The king gloried in pride with his extravagantly ostentatious display of luxury—the *Barge's* richly designed mahogany interiors and her fine fittings and furnishings—built four years before at a cost of $50,000. But wooden ships have a way of deteriorating and finally going to pieces. Even as the ship's owners began demanding their payment of cut sandalwood, the grand ship's timbers were discovered to be rotting away. The *Barge* met its fate in four more years, wrecked on the north shore of Kauai.

Compared to this prize of great price, the purchase of the *Thaddeus*, that had borne to Hawaii the pioneer company of missionaries and then made another long voyage back to Hawaii from New England, was a great opportunity. Liholiho grabbed up such a bargain, getting in addition a schooner, *Young Thaddeus*, built in Hawaii, all for only half the cost of the ill-fated *Barge*.

But, alas, the king had picked another lemon. His plan to use the *Thaddeus* for inter-island trading went plop on the first trip, as the ship was then so unseaworthy as to have barely made it back to port. And so the historic *Thaddeus* was allowed to go to pieces on the beach at Honolulu.

Until the traders became so voraciously eager for it, this fragrant wood had represented no great value to Hawaiians. They called it *iliahi* and used it to make themselves smell better, by grinding up the heart of this wood and using this powder to give a pleasant scent to their tapa clothes. Then the American trading ship captains discovered the eager market for sandalwood in the Orient. There its fragrant wood was valued for making incense, fans and other small items, and salves with supposed medicinal qualities.

Some wood was gathered on Kauai in 1790 and 1791. By 1805 the profitable trade in sandalwood was in full swing and tempting both traders and producers. Wise Kamehameha came to realize the bonanza he had in these trees and took over control of the trading. Having an eye to the future, he also restricted the cutting of small trees. Kamehameha bought the ship *Columbia* in 1817, paying for it as Kelolo did with "twice the full of the vessel." By the time he died in 1819, the trade was flourishing, its profits filling the coffers of American merchantmen, and their extravagantly priced products puffing up regal pride and piling up in royal warehouses.

The chiefs learned to live lavishly and, instead of paying off their mounting debts, incurred more with promissory notes, and kept on amassing the tempting goods the clever salesman offered. Days of reckoning fell upon them in due time. American warships came in 1826 to enforce the demands for payment being cried for by the over-zealous Yankee traders. The Hawaiian government had to foot most of the bill by assessing in that year its first written tax, to be paid in sandalwood or Spanish dollars, mats or tapa. This sent the burdened natives off again to hunt down the little remaining pieces of sandalwood in the forests. By 1829 the sandalwood was practically depleted.

Boki, governor of Oahu, was still direly in debt then. So ambitious and desperate was he that, when word was brought to him of sandalwood treasures in the New Hebrides, he loaded two ships with men, arms and ammunition to set up a trading colony there. Victim of a storm—or the wrath of the Lord, as the missionaries could well believe—the ship that Boki was on never made it to its destination, lost at sea; and the other ship finally managed to limp back to Honolulu with only 20 of about 500 members of the expedition surviving dreadful illness and starvation.

Clearing off the sandalwood forests was a national disaster. Not only the wastefulness and debt problems afflicted the country, but the physical condition of the people was sadly weakened by such demanding labor. Kuykendall cites an occasion similar to the scene Abner Hale witnessed: "2,000 persons, laden with faggots of sandalwood,...wearied with their unpaid labours."

Another citation by the Reverend Peter Gulick of Kauai in 1830 records: "Felt distressed and grieved for the people who collect sandalwood;" and he tells how they had to subsist on "wild and bitter herbs, moss, & c.," and, clad only in the native malo, labor on in such cold weather that Gulick felt scarcely comfortable in his winter clothes.

As the people neglected their fields, they failed to raise crops to feed themselves. At one time, near famine threatened. Straining themselves so vigorously and being undernourished, they more quickly gave in to the new diseases cutting down the population. They were being sacrificed for the chiefs' selfish satisfactions.

Thus greed brought on such ill effects to a young, struggling nation. Today only minor and remote remnants of sandalwood remain in Hawaii.

XIV. "SEE NO EVIL, HEAR NO EVIL, SPEAK NO EVIL"

Abner Hale "loved the Hawaiians, yet he despised them." Within his private domain, the Hawaiian language is kapu, lest his children be given this key to knowledge and "learn the ways of the heathen." His children are kept strictly apart from the native offspring, for Abner fears for them the "inherent danger from too close relationships with the Hawaiian savages."

So "it was under the impetus of this fear that he built a high wall around his entire establishment....Within the wall not a word of Hawaiian was spoken." Jerusha conducts her classes in an open shed outside the wall. When Hawaiians come to consult the missionary, Abner would take them to "the native room" and "carefully close the door to where his children were."

♣ ♣ ♣

Such were the fears and consequent fervent aim of the missionaries to protect their dear children from being exposed to native corruption of the "low and vile examples around them," as Bingham corroborates.

Daniel and Jerusha Chamberlain had sacrificed all their wealth and comfort and come out on this soul-saving expedition with no qualms about such dangers for their five children. Their two older boys had attended the Foreign Mission School at Cornwall, Conn., and, on reaching Hawaii, they "learned to speak Hawaiian very readily and gave valuable service as interpreters for the missionaries." Whether their young minds became dangerously polluted by such contacts with the savages does not appear in the records.

First warnings of such possible results from missionary children getting on familiar terms with their native counterparts came from English missionaries from Tahiti, who visited Hawaii in 1823. From their 30 years of experience with the Polynesians there, they strenuously advised the American missionaries: "Let Mr. and Mrs. Chamberlain take their six children (one born in Hawaii), go home and train them up for God. They never can do it here. As society now is, for unformed characters to come in contact with natives as foreigners, is moral death."

So, with Daniel Chamberlain suffering from health problems and finding he was unable to develop agriculture as expected, the family, with the approval of the others, returned home to provide a good safe education for their children. Those who remained never forgot these dire warnings and sacrificed much to protect their young ones from the sinful ways of their adopted land.

Lucy Thurston particularly dwelt repeatedly on the subject in her letters and records. But, hardy spirit that she was, she alone labored not only to carry on her expected missionary duties but to keep her children under her strict supervision, providing in her home their good education until at the age of 16 and 18 she could take them back to New England for advance study.

The other missionaries sacrificed themselves and their children by sending the little ones back to relatives and friends to have them brought up and educated in the sound foundation of their good old New England and its purely safe environment. Bingham explains the policy he and the others followed: "It was the general opinion of the missionaries...that their children over 8 and 10 years of age, notwithstanding the trial that might be involved, ought to be sent or carried to the United States...that they might escape the dangers of a heathen country, and inherit a portion of the civil, religious, and literary privileges which their ancestors had bequeathed them, and at the same time allow the parents more time and strength for missionary work."

Bingham knew well whereof he spoke. Relating the fearful experiences of his own daughter, he wrote in a letter to the American Board, "We fled with our first born from the war on Kauai, we carried her asleep into Mr. Richards' cellar when Lahaina was fired upon—but we could not easily hush her cries when I and my house were mob'd at Honolulu, nor will she soon lose the impression that we are here in continual danger from the assaults of wicked men."

Titus Coan later wrote about this "trial of painful character" that these early missionaries had to bear to see that their children were reared "in a land of schools and churches and Christian civilization. The struggle of parting has sometimes been agonizing on both sides. Often the child would plead piteously to be suffered to remain, while at the same time the mother's heart yearned for her darling one; but a stern sense of duty nerved her to the sacrifice, and with a kiss of farewell she would commit her son or daughter to the care of the ship-master, and turn away with a crushed heart to spend sleep-less hours in prayers and tears."

It was anguish for the Reverend Richard Armstrong to part with his daughter, sadly one of the last of the missionary children to be shipped off because of lack of proper education in Hawaii. After the heart-rending parting, he wrote in his diary that the brig *Flora* had carried away "my own dear child, my first born, the beginning of my strength—my Caroline." Laura Judd recorded the scene of painful leave-taking of this "little girl, not more than 7 years old, standing on the deck and looking at her father on shore. She stretched out her little arms toward him and shrieked with all of her strength, 'Oh father, dear father, do take me back.'" A year later Punahou School opened for the education of missionary children.

Meanwhile, refusing to tear her children away from her loving care and personal instruction and discipline, Lucy Thurston devised and maintained the separation of her children from native contamination with a schedule to keep them busy, happy and learning the true values of life that every faithful missionary's child should know. It was she who arranged her household, as Abner Hale does, to shut her children off from all knowledge of Hawaiian speech and so from the natives' too-common reference to the facts of life.

About a third of a mile from the shore at Kailua, the Thurstons established their home to make arrangements for their "double responsibilities required, of molding heathen society, and of forming the character of our children." They enclosed five acres with a stone wall three feet wide and six feet high. Inside their large thatched house was "the reception room for natives." Not a step farther could they proceed "without permission or invitation." This room was also Asa's study.

Another large room served as dining room, with small thatched cookhouse beyond, where their household natives worked. In that dining room Lucy conducted school for the natives. A hall in back led to the only entrance to a three-acre yard, where stood another house, the children's home, with family sitting room and bedrooms.

As Lucy often invited her native friends into her sitting room, her children could then go out through the back bedroom into their own private play yard, while Lucy enjoyed "the satisfied feeling of their being safe, beyond the reach of native influence."

"The first rule to be attended to with regard to children," Lucy firmly declared, "is that they must not speak the native language." The mother must see that this law be not violated, and she must "form in her children fixed habits of doing as they are required. No intercourse whatever should exist between children and heathen." Lucy was strongly determined to insure her children's virtue and provide for their future usefulness.

Lucy had to solve another problem in her children's isolation. As her daughter grew older, she began to rebel against having to walk in the hot sun to church, sit "in a crowded assembly, for the sake of being within sounds she could neither understand, nor was allowed to utter." Her father's preaching was in fluent Hawaiian. Back home after such a long, tiring service, she would cry and demand, "Mama, what do I go to church for?" So mama arranged for her children to stay home for an "hour dedicated to religious instruction in our own language."

In the children's home schooling, Asa taught sacred music and Latin. Lucy gave instruction in grammar, geography, history, arithmetic and philosophy, using clock and bell to divide the day into "half hour diversions." Thus Lucy consoled herself that she was not delivering her own children over to Satan, while still tending "to the labor of bringing back a revolted race to the service of Jehovah" in her native school work.

Unfortunate in one respect was such isolation of youth and its freedom of spirit. Aboard ship on her way to America, Lucy's daughter Lucy found a life of gayety refreshingly enjoyable—something she had never experienced before. At the same time, she felt conscience-stricken that she should allow herself to laugh so freely. She wrote in her diary, "I am ashamed of myself many times a day for giving way to so much laughter, but there are so many witty remarks made, that it is almost impossible to refrain from it. I have heard more jokes, hyperbolic expressions and comical remarks on board, than I did during 17 years of my residence at the Sandwich Islands."

Then, thinking back to her heavy religious training, she became apologetic for her carefree attitude and enjoyment of life. "I feel I have parted far from God and my duty, since being on board,..." she later confessed, "not favorable to growth in grace...no retired place for meditation and prayer, I feel I have dishonored my Savior."

Unhappily, poor Lucy was not destined to revel in such happiness, as her life was cut short soon after her arrival at New York. Her mother, at her dear daughter's bedside, rejoiced in the girl's strong religious spirit. She with deep sense of satisfaction reported, "Many precious words fell from her lips, and her feelings were characterized by sweet submission to the Divine will, and an unshaken reliance on the Savior." Now this mother could boast, "Four children on earth and one in heaven!"

XV. The Ghosts Of Hawaii

One of Abner's most mystifying experiences is his rescue from the awful power of "the revengeful night watchers," when the terrified Kelolo hurls him over a hedge into a foul water ditch to save him. There, drenched and soiled, Abner witnesses Kelolo's stupefying fear of unseen forces. The chief manages to describe the dreadful scene of "the great alii of the past" marching threateningly upon him:

"They carry torches and feathered staves. They wear the golden robes and feather helmets. Maku Hale, they are coming for me." In his agony, Kelolo implores Pele to be their savior, and the goddess complies. The heavy wind dies down, and that strange sound of marching feet dissipates. Abner just can't understand and explain the weird situation he had to suffer through.

♠ ♠ ♠

From his knowledge of Hawaiian lore, Michener has here concocted a missionary tale without parallel. If the men of God heard such tales, they would naturally consider them just part of "the darkness of unmitigated superstition," Bingham refers to, of those "ignorant and fearful" heathens.

Though this spooky part of the old Hawaiian religion went underground when Christianity dominated, such tales survive and come to light. Only the family god, such as Kelolo's Pele, or a relative can turn away the threatening spear of a marching chief in such visitations from the home of the dead. Not only the sound of footsteps may be heard, but also, perhaps, chanting or drum beats as the night marchers push relentlessly onward.

Two such personal experiences with the night marchers were related in the 1971 Holloween edition of the Sunday *Star-Bulletin* & *Advertiser* under the heading "My Favorite Ghost Story."

Napua Stevens Poire, prominent proponent of Hawaiian culture, told of her frightening experience as a young girl encountering the night marchers during a visit to her great-great-grand-aunt at Kohala on the Big Island. A dirge-like chant of welcome had called upon the spirits of the family members buried nearby to join in the grand-aunt's hospitality and blessings. That set up frightening feelings among the younger set. Forbidding rules emphasized the constraints upon them.

One restriction was that they must not play down in that attractive grassy, meadow-like section of land. But, when grand-aunt departed to visit relatives, down the road the children dashed and began frolicking about in reckless abandon to enjoy their freedom.

Suddenly a howling wind assailed Napua's ears, and she "heard heavy footsteps, the beating of drums, the murmur of voices." And then she realized she had been left alone. Terrified, she stood there, unable to move, unable to cry out. And "the drums drummed louder," she told, "and the sound of marching feet was practically on me. I heard again the murmur of voices that had become loud chants. Suddenly, without warning, I was shoved rudely off the path into the high grass." And she heard a Hawaiian name whispered.

Recovering, she ran fast back to the house, sobbing in her fright. When she became calm enough to tell what had happened, her grand-aunt explained she had strayed "into the path reserved for those who are permitted to roam the earth, those who are called the 'night marchers.'" She had been saved by one of her family "in a gesture of love and concern for a relative."

The other story was from Emma de Fries, guide at the Queen Emma Summer Palace in Nuuanu, a great-great-granddaughter of Hewahewa, kahuna nui (high priest) of Kamehameha I.

Her tale was of the amazing scene witnessed by the Chinese laborers on the rice plantation of her grandfather, Henry de Fries, at Hanalei, Kauai. While preparing the paddies, they were frightened off by the sight of "hundreds of men walking down from the mountains on a trail near the Hanalei River. The marchers were dressed in malos and short feathered capes and all of them carried spears."

At this threatening advance, the workers ran away, then, looking back, they gazed in disbelief at beholding the warriors "walking through a stone wall that ran the length of the road. Afterwards, they disappeared in the Hanalei River."

Such are the mysteries of the religion. All the old Hawaiian beliefs have not vanished entirely under the rule of Christ and Almighty God.

XVI. CHURCHES—VICTIMS OF FIRE AND WHIRLWIND

Abner's struggle with Kelolo and the kahunas over the structure of his precious new church impresses many readers. Some try to apply the tale to Mokuaikaua Church rather than to the one in Lahaina where Abner was stationed.

Kelolo's men took four years to put up Abner's "sprawling edifice." The style was that of early native church buildings: "a perfect rectangle with handsomely matted grass walls…and not a shred of furniture except one wooden bench for Jerusha and Captain Janders. The multitude, more than 3,000 of them, spread individual pandanus mats on the pebbled floor and sat tailor fashion, elbow to elbow."

Abner's planning problem is his obstinate opposition to the kahunas' unbroken belief that he is having the door of the church in the wrong place "for the spirits of this location." But Abner is adamant in his assurance that his church in Hawaii must look like the churches in New England and those in Europe, "built foursquare" with high walls instead of allowing open space for air to circulate. And so, "with no air stirring, the congregation [sat] sweltering in the natural heat, plus the radiation of 3,000 closely packed bodies."

Then rampaging sailors, rioting against the new laws depriving them of their accustomed pleasures, pitch burning torches onto the grass roofing and the peoples' "beloved church" goes up in flames. Malama, "by her daring charm," manages to wheedle enough money from the ships' captains to allow Abner to realize another of his dreams: the Seamen's Chapel at Lahaina—"a place to read, and pray, and write letters home to their dear ones."

Abner's church is rebuilt in the same design, although the kahunas know it is doomed to destruction again. Sure enough. "The wind howled down from the mountains...rising to...furious levels, sending the church roof hurtling aloft and then tearing down the walls."

Then, for the third time, the church structure is completed and the kahunas set the door in the right place, "and the famous stone church they built that year stood for more than a century."

✦ ✦ ✦

The first church in Lahaina was quickly erected within three months after the arrival of the first missionaries there in 1823. Bingham describes it as of "ordinary structure, frail materials" and "of moderate dimensions." No matter how simple and fragile it was, Bingham exulted that "in its spiritual design, it was not inferior to the most costly and superb churches in Christendom."

This church served about eight years. Governor Hoapili, with some aid from other chiefs, then had the first stone church in Hawaii built between 1828 and 1832. Dr. Dwight Baldwin, who served at Lahaina from 1835 to 1870, records that this church was "two stories high with galleries, to seat 3,000 people in the native manner, close together on the floor." It provided also calabash spitoons for the convenience of tobacco-chewing chiefs and ships' masters.

Hoapili named the church Ebenezer, later changed to Wainee. This building weakened within 16 years, leaving only two thirds of the original wall. That section was rebuilt and shingled and a higher steeple added to make it conform "to the general style of churches in the United States." Then came the terrible whirlwind of 1858 to rip off the steeple and half the roof.

Fire destroyed the church again in 1894, when royalists, rioting over annexation of their country by the United States, took vengeance on it. The church was rebuilt and dedicated less than three years later. But, in 1947, sparks from a rubbish fire set it in flames once again and it had to be repaired. Then down swooped the Kauaula wind again at 80 miles an hour to lift the church up in the air and dump it in a heap.

What had gone amiss? Perhaps it was misnamed. Wainee means "moving water." Rebuilt in 1953, it was rechristened Waiola—Water of Life.

Lahaina's missionaries did also provide for the comfort and edification of the visiting seamen, for not all were tipplers and women-chasers. William Richards and Ephraim Spaulding in 1834 got the ships' officers to support their project of arranging for reading rooms and a retreat from the heat and dust of the town. This earthen building was replaced in two years by a stone building "two stories high, the lower part...devoted to sundry purposes of the mission and to a reading-room for seamen," the upper floor reserved as "a seamen's chapel and vestry." Dwight Baldwin in 1841 had "an adobe structure for a seamen's chapel built at the back of the mission premises."

Disaster struck other early churches, requiring the building of four successive churches in Honolulu in seven years. A native deliberately burned down the first church three years after it had been built, finishing the job a white man had attempted previously by throwing "a lighted cigar into the tinder of the thatching."

The chiefs saw to it that this native church was promptly rebuilt. Another church put up just a year and a half later succumbed to a violent rain storm. A large temporary house followed, and then in 1829 Bingham rejoiced in a new "commodious house of worship, 63 feet wide and stretching 196 feet to seat 3,000 to 4,000 Hawaiians. Two very large doors at each end and as many smaller ones on the sides" received the crowd of worshipers. This building served until the present Kawaiahao Church was completed in 1842, after six years spent in its construction.

The Reverend Elias Bond, who struggled along bravely at his Kohala mission, suffered among other troubles having his new church demolished.

When he had arrived in 1841 at this isolated station, a region of steep cliffs and deep valleys often made miserable by high winds and drenching rains, the church he found was "very rotten and leaky everywhere, a wallowing place of hogs during the week."

For three years the people toiled to build a more substantial church, cutting trees in the mountains, taking them by schooner up the coast, and then bearing them ten miles on their backs. For only four years could they enjoy this "Sanctuary of God" before a violent gale left it a pile of broken timbers and rubbish in 1849. Nothing daunted, the people again banded together to build the present stone church, with stones from the gulches, coral clumps from 20 to 30 feet deep in the sea, sand from the distant shores, all lugged on strong shoulders up hill to the building site. The Herculean task was completed in 1855.

Kailua, blessed with "the largest and most elegant native building ever erected in Hawaii," as its second church in 1826, saw this one go by the hand of another incendiary nine years later. The missionaries, sailing for Honolulu, saw from their ship "the flames ascending to the heavens." A mighty building effort then put up the present stone wall church in 13 months.

XVII. Defying The Evildoers

The glory of Lahaina fades in the Hales' view when the whalers arrive in force and the girls welcome them with open legs. Abner knows the town is just "the modern Sodom and Gomorrah," a port for "open debauchery." It takes some time for him to convince Malama she must make strict laws and enforce them to prevent such flourishing evils. At first she puts aside the idea with "I think you missionaries want to stop all fun." But, convinced of the dangers, she marches to the pier and proclaims, "Sailors shall not roam the streets at night. Girls shall not swim out to the whaling ships."

One captain mutters, "There'll be hell to pay for this." Then he adds, "God help the missionary."

That night some 50 men gather at the mission house, cursing Abner Hale and threatening to "hang the little bastard" or "burn his damned house down." But they hold back from doing any more than hurling "vile insults" and a "storm of rocks" at his grass house.

Next night the sailors get drunk and decide to burn the church down. Outraged at that dastardly act, the "big natives crashed down upon" every errant sailor they could find.

Then comes raging in, the demon himself, Captain Hoxworth, damns the new laws and roars to the restrained sailors they can go get "whiskey, girls, any damned thing you want." He puts on a terrifying scene at the Hales' "really miserable hovel," finally leaves, threatening to blow their house to pieces from a cannon on a ship in the harbor. He carries out his threat, knocks out the gate to the fort, then directs his firing at the mission house. The rioting kept up for three days.

✿ ✿ ✿

In the fall of 1825, Queen Kaahumanu got the law broadcast in the ports of Honolulu and Lahaina that girls would not be permitted to go off to the waiting ships in the harbor. Guards patrolled the shore to arrest any female attempting to evade these new restrictions. Loomis records that one girl, happily "swimming off toward a whaler, was pursued, captured and put in irons." The chiefs "had her shorn and fettered and displayed in all the villages."

Deprived of their "rights," the female-fond sailors soon became desperate with desire and determined to make forceful demands for the restitution of their accustomed form of "rest and relaxation" after their strenuous way of life of "hardship and toil."

Loomis cites the case of 20 English whalers who assailed Bingham to know the cause of such an unfair prohibition. The missionary sent them to Kaahumanu for an answer. She told them such ways were wicked and must be stopped and threatened to have them punished if they broke the peace.

The first big revolt of seamen was at Lahaina, where William Richards staunchly guarded his followers' morals. A ship's crew came ashore with eager expectations, having had the run of the town and the pick of the female populace on a previous visit. Their captain had then acquired a permanent partner for his bunk for $160. Now all such privileges were kapu.

In retaliation, men marched to Richards's mission house to unleash "a succession of fearful threats and gross insults," demanding either freed females or a fatal end to the missionary. Richards stoutly refused.

From the ship they returned later in three boats and "armed with knives and pistols" to enforce their demand. Infuriated by his refusals, these savage sailors seemed about "to execute their horrid threats" when "Mrs. Richards, with the spirit of a martyr, rushed between them and her husband, exclaiming, 'My only protection is in my husband and my God; I had hoped the helplessness of a female, surrounded only by heathen, would have touched the compassion of men from a Christian land!" She assured the belligerent crowd that she was willing to lay down her life "sooner than…countenancing in the people we have come to enlighten, a course of conduct at variance with the word of God.'"

That brave speech deterred the men and they withdrew for a while but returned "with a more relentless determination," until the natives did interfere "to rescue the lives of their teachers at the hazard of their own."

Three thousand men took up arms to protect the missionaries against another attempt at such an outrage. They loaded the cannon in the fort, ready to fire upon the ship if need be. Not taking such a chance, the captain sailed off to Honolulu in quest of the men's goals. But guards there were ready for them to prevent trouble.

Unfortunately the next aggressive attempt to invalidate the effects of the new moral laws was by the commander of the first American warship to arrive in Hawaii. He was Lieutenant John "Mad Jack" Percival. "He soon made known his views of the restraints on vile women," Bingham notes, appealing to the high chiefs for a redress of the grievance presented by his crew. Kaahumanu prepared a statement that Bingham felt sufficient "to meet the strange pretence that an embargo on lewd women, at the islands, was an insult to the U.S. flag!" She asserted her right to control her own subjects and declared that foreign visitors to a country are bound to conform to its laws.

To this, "Mad Jack" sent a reply that he would come to talk but he would shoot Bingham if he came. The chiefs granted Percival an audience with Kaahumanu and the young King Kauikeaouli, the joint rulers. To them he protested that it was Bingham who said to "tabu the women" and that his men would come to get women, and, if they did not get them, they would fight. After a long exchange of words, Kaahumanu finally told the blustering captain that the only reasonable objection he could have against the tabu of women would be if he had brought American women with him and the chiefs had put a tabu on them.

Frustrated, "he snapped his fingers in rage, and clenched his fists, and said, 'To-morrow I will give my men rum: look out: they will come for women; and if they don't get them they will fight...If the women are not released from tabu to-morrow, my people will come and tear down the houses of the missionaries.'"

Repeating that threat, about 150 men from ships invaded the house of the high chief Kalanimoku, where other chiefs were to meet that Sunday afternoon. "Thus commenced a riot," Bingham relates, "which occupied the time and place of the expected divine service. They were followed by successive squads. One and another dashed in the windows of Kalanimoku's fine hall, breaking some 70 panes along the verandah."

Seeing a mob heading for his house, Hiram dashed home by a different route, only to find himself locked out and leaving him in the hands of the rioters. One fellow dashed in the windows of his house. Others held Bingham with their clubs pressed against him. He called to the natives for help but managed to get away from his assailants and run back to the chief's enclosure.

His Hawaiian friends nearby promised they would "take care" of him. They were just reluctant to take part in any action until forcible aid was really needed. That occasion developed right then. Suddenly Bingham saw one sailor strike "a spiteful blow with a club at my head, which was warded off, partly by the arm of Lydia Namahana, and partly by my umbrella. It was the signal for resistance, for which the natives had waited. They sprang upon the rioters; some they seized, disarmed, and bound, and to some they dealt leveling blows." Bingham's Christian compassion saved one sailor's life. Seeing him clubbed down "like an ox at the slaughter," the missionary "felt the bowels of tenderness move, and entreated the natives not to kill the foreigners."

Rushing back home and gaining entrance now, Bingham soon found sailors back there at the attack. "One broke in a window; another beat with violence against the door; two applied their strength to force it." The fortunate arrival of Lieut. Percival and some of his officers providentially prevented further destruction, as the commander started using "his cane over some of the turbulent men."

After this fracas, the commander, admitting his men "had gone too far," again posed his objections to the tabu to the chiefs. The more tolerant Governor Boki yielded, and boatloads of women again rode out to the ships in the harbor, much to the dismay of the missionaries. Percival attempted to mollify them somewhat by requesting ships' captains to allow "but a small proportion" of their crews to go on shore at the same time, thus "preventing anxiety to the missionary family." He also "ordered the repair of Kalanimoku's house" and also Bingham's, and "put in irons two men who had assailed [Bingham] with knife and club."

The missionary physician, Dr. Abraham Blatchley, took care of the sailors' wounds. The warship continued in port for the rest of its three months' visit, referred to as "the mischief-making man-of-war." Advised of the outrage Percival had caused, the American Board requested the United States to investigate the affair. Bingham was pleased that the Court of Inquiry found abundant evidence to back the complaints. In the Sandwich Islands this flagrant example of misconduct strongly influenced the high chiefs to feel "the importance of attempting to free their country from the terrible evils of licentiousness and intemperance."

At Lahaina, later that year, the crews of several English and American whaleships threatened to kill William Richards because he had influenced the prohibition against prostitution. They went to demolish his home, but the natives carefully guarded it. Richards was then at Kailua on Hawaii and stayed there six weeks until it was safe to return.

More menacing mischief was scheduled in poor Richards' almanac. Here come the cannon balls!

Ignoring the law and evading the guards, several girls made their way to a ship in Lahaina harbor. Governor Hoapili requested the captain to return these girls and kept on insisting for several days, without result. Hoapili's strategem then was to haul up on the shore the captain's boat after he came ashore. The captain called upon Richards for help, and the missionary agreed to help him if he would promise to return the girls.

Aboard ship, the men learned that their captain was being held. Their ire flared so high they started firing their cannon at the town, by no means accidentally landing shells in the mission yard. With more direct success, the whalers might have eliminated both of their hatred deniers of their pleasures. For the Binghams were visiting the Richards family, and all had to hustle themselves and their children down into the cellar to save their lives from threatened destruction. Luckily the captain arrived back on ship in time to put a stop to the cannon blasts, and then sailed for Honolulu—with the girls still aboard.

Such was the life of the missionaries who sought to bring this life-saving morality to these people who had, without fear of the Lord, innocently been enjoying themselves, offering their physical hospitality to strangers, and, in doing so, bringing on their own destruction. They were just learning the wide differences between men seeking only their own satisfaction and those whose efforts aimed for the higher rewards of life through rightful conduct.

XVIII. Beware Of The Backsliders

Cautious and self-assured Abner Hale was not one to allow any but a carefully selected few of those "deceitful and licentious" Hawaiians to become members of his church of God. This shocks Dr. Whipple to find such meager progress in the number of conversions. "In all these years," he accuses Abner, "you've allowed nine people to join your church as full members. Somewhere, Abner, you've gone wrong."

Abner's excuse is "It takes time to convert the heathen to true [religion]." For Abner is convinced he can not afford to forget his setback when the supposedly converted sailor aboard the *Thetis* failed to hold the faith. That became the "one fundamental lesson" Abner absorbed on the long trip: that "the established church must not be maneuvered into a position of danger by the backsliding of fools who were never truly saved in the first place. l was too prompt to accept this man...too eager for merely another number rather than for a secured soul. We must never repeat this foolish mistake in Hawaii."

So Abner becomes imbued with the compelling belief that backsliders are the ones "more than sinners, who damage the church." Malama is such a problem to Abner. He struggles in debates with her over the absolute need for accepting and following God's word, never yielding to her entreaties to be accepted into church membership through baptism until she is finally humble and contrite on her death bed.

♠ ♠ ♠

Hiram Bingham and the other missionaries were also extremely cautious about baptizing natives, even the high chiefs, and taking them into their holy churches before they had thoroughly proved themselves willing and able to bow to God's will without backsliding into their heathen ways. It was not until the chiefs had been "five years under the inspection and instruction of the missionaries, who had seen them in their heathen pollution and wretchedness" that they were permitted to come before the church and make "a statement of their religious views, and their desire to join themselves to the Lord's people, and to walk in his covenant."

Bingham was pleased to count ten of the highest chiefs in the land among these first ones to fulfill the rigid demands of the church's stern rulers. These ignorant savages must bow before God and express "their repentance for sin, their love of God, their reliance on Christ, their satisfaction in prayer, their desire to forsake the ways of iniquity and death, and to obey the gospel." By then they were ready to agree to tread "the path…narrow and straight, leading through great self-denial and many difficulties, requiring vigilance and perseverance, the renunciation and abandonment of much of what is valued by the world but is unfavorable to the interests of the soul."

Before Kaahumanu could be eligible for inclusion among these select of the Lord, she had to forego her earlier prerogative of enjoying the royal prince of Kauai as her extra husband, since Bingham declared, "Paul would not allow such a relation to exist in a church under his supervision."

Yet, even after these rigid demands for their moral enrichment had been met and their acceptance of them publicly manifested, the missionaries "still hesitated to baptize them, until as candidates they were set before the church and the world for the trial of a few months more, under watchful missionary care and instruction." It did not matter, as Bingham admitted, that "they had [already], for several months at least, given much evidence of conversion." Later, Bingham explains, "Often were multitudes held back from uniting with the church on the ground that it could do them no good, unless they were truly converted, though they might think themselves to be the true disciples of Christ."

At Kailua too, the Thurstons watched, as Lucy reported in 1830, "this neglected portion of our race, groping along in the darkness of nature, listening to messages from heaven with indifference and contempt." Then she happily saw "a secret energy was transforming their moral characters" and these "slaves of all the sins which degrade human nature" were "now sitting at the feet of Jesus, learning and doing his will." Until 1828 "no native at Kailua had been baptized," she admitted, proudly adding, "Since that time 65 have been admitted to the Holy Communion, and a much larger number give evidence of having experienced the renovating influence of the Spirit."

Though the natives flocked to the new churches, the membership rolls looked rather slim throughout the first 17 years, with less than 1,300 persons winning divine acceptance through the human harvest of missionary efforts throughout the island chain. The people were not deemed to have reached the high degree of benevolence Puritan standards demanded of them. The trouble was, Daniel Chamberlain made clear in 1831, that these willing church-goers had "so little of that deep feeling of sinfulness and unworthyness, which a correct knowledge of the human heart and a clear discovery of the character of God always produces."

The American Board, feeling its missionaries were perhaps dragging their feet too much in their unwillingness to accept converts, suggested they might be using an excessive degree of caution. They advised that the missionaries' own high personal "standards by which to judge piety, cannot be the one for the Sandwich Islands, nor any heathen country."

This gave way to a more easy-going policy and allowed the "great revival" to sweep over the isles for three years from 1837. Church membership boomed then, with nearly 20,000 added to the rolls. The impetus to this rich harvesting of souls came after the arrival of the largest of the missionary companies in 1837, when a party of 32 came to bolster the work of the Lord.

The leaders of this massing of saved sinners were two extraordinarily efficacious evangelists whose devotion and zeal met no match in other sections of the islands. The Reverend Lorenzo Lyons, famous for his excellent hymn writing, at Waimea on Hawaii first won recognition for his powers of oratory in winning the heathen to God.

Even outdoing Lyons's accomplishments was the grandiloquent Titus Coan at Hilo. He could transfix his congregation with fiery words in his eager religious emotion. Both men received hundreds of natives to be baptized for admission to their churches. It became almost a mania to build manpower for the service of God.

Those on other islands took up the call to bring in the waiting souls, though with not such overflowing success. Indeed some, like the more down-to-earth William Richards, felt that those exciting the multitudes to confessing their sins and coming to be saved might be overdoing the cause and going to the other extreme by not holding their converts on probation for a due period. After the revival had spent its course in three years, the corralling of confessed sinners slowed down to a more normal pace.

Kuykendall concludes that in spite of "much superficiality, particularly in many of the conversions during the revival," and a "full quota of 'backsliders'" in the Hawaiian churches, plus "innumerable instances of the survival of 'idolatrous' and 'heathenish' beliefs and practices,…the record is full of examples of sincere and consistent Christian piety and good conduct, and the Hawaiian churches can point with pride to" the character of many of their leading chiefs. "By 1840," Kuykendall believes, "Hawaii was officially a Christian nation."

XIX. KEEP OUT THOSE IDOLATROUS CATHOLICS

Aboard the *Thetis*, Abner had struggled with his conscience over the temptations of "sanctified joy" so freely offered him by Jerusha. His one great self-reassuring thought in this matter is that the celibacy that the Catholic priests had to subscribe to was "nothing but popery, and if there was one thing he wished with all his heart to avoid it was popish ways." Mulling over thoughts of abstinence from the temptations of the flesh, he comes to reject such a course emphatically with "No! That is the Romish way!"

Later, when Abner is determinedly trying to convince Malama that she is headed straight for the tortures of hellfire, she remembers a Catholic sea captain and inquires, "Are Catholics in the fire too?"

"They are in the fire forever," Abner replies with absolute conviction.

No Catholic priests come to plague Abner. He has enough troubles without having to suffer conflict with Popish invaders within his religious realm in Michener's story.

❧ ❧ ❧

Hawaii's missionaries did face this threatening competitive problem. They too had inculcated in the chiefs' mind a hatred and fear of Catholic subversion in their newly cherished religious sphere. The leaders of the nation then entertained no such tolerance, acceptance and understanding of this other, different faith, as did Governor Kuakini in Kona later, when the animosities had subsided somewhat.

The strongly Puritan men from New England enjoyed seven secure years for their indoctrination of the chiefs before the first threat to their monopoly on divine truth came. It was 1827 when the first Catholic priests arrived in Honolulu with some lay brothers and agricultural settlers.

Bingham wondered just what course to pursue. He pondered "whether it is right to bid God speed or not to a system of teaching which forbids free access to the Bible, and is subversive of the Gospel," or whether the government should "appear indifferent or neutral in respect to [such] alien teachers." His fears and prejudices won out, and he stoutly backed Kaahumanu's refusal "to receive or admit the Papal teachers."

He cited "the boasted oneness and infallibility of the Romish church from the days of her departure from the standard of Christ [which] make her responsible for all the dogmas, superstitions, and idolatries, which she has once authorized and never renounced." He warned that "the delusions, follies, and sins of men" in this faith would bring in "a new superstition or fatal error among the Hawaiians, or the almost certain means of civil dissensions."

The trick was how to get rid of these opposing interlopers. The priests cleverly kept avoiding the use of all proffered means for their deportation.

For the first year and a half, they contented themselves with learning the language. By the end of two years, they had only 65 adult converts and some children.

Bingham became alarmed as he saw "the Romanists at Honolulu... erecting or enlarging their buildings [and] inculcating the Romish faith" and as he observed that the people "who received their images and pictures, professed to worship a God different from him whom the Christian chiefs and their missionaries worshiped...a French or Papal deity." Kaahumanu, well imbued with Bingham's assurance that Catholics would undermine the nation, finally managed to ship the priests off to California late in 1831.

Active in the protection of the missionaries' now eagerly accepted Protestantism, the regent Kaahumanu, and later Kinau, punished those of their people who tended to stray from the fold and turn to what these chiefs considered to be, according to their teaching, the evils of idolatry. Catholic-worshiping natives were sent to jail and subjected to forced labor.

Never at a loss for words, Bingham devotes pages in his book to his accusations against the Catholics. He happily supports his case by quoting from an "address of Congress at Philadelphia, 1774," urging the people of Great Britain to refrain from allowing Catholic emigrants from Europe to "reduce the ancient free Protestant colony [of Canada] to a state of slavery," since this religion had previously "deluged your island in blood, and dispersed impiety, bigotry, persecution, murder, and re-bellion throughout every part of the world."

With this removal of the Catholic priests, the mis-sionaries gained five more years of freedom from Popish insurgency, until France sent another priest to Hawaii in 1836. But the Hawaiian chiefs were adamant against any teaching of Catholic doctrine in their strictly Protestant realm. Then the two priests previously expelled to Cali-fornia slipped back to Honolulu the following year. Their presence brought on much dissension among French and British officials and the government for about three months. After this extensive flow of accusations, defenses and explanations, the final agreement allowed these two priests to stay until they could arrange for passage to more welcome shores. The other priest was permitted to re-main, but all priests were prohibited from preaching and teaching their religion to native Hawaiians as long as they were in residence.

The two priests finally left in November. One of them was Father Bachelot, who, in 1828, had planted on the grounds of the Catholic mission in Honolulu the seed of an algaroba tree which he had brought from the Royal Gardens in Paris. It grew into the tree known in Hawaii as the kiawe and on the mainland as the mesquite. It be-came valuable for its flowers as a source of honey, its pods as fodder for cattle, and its hard wood for charcoal. As he was about to leave, Father Bachelot prophesied, "As this tree has grown and spread, so will the Catholic religion grow and spread in these Islands."

In December the king issued a decree forbidding the teaching of "the peculiarities of the Pope's religion" in Hawaii or of allowing any ship "from bringing any teacher of that religion into this kingdom."

Aroused by the expulsion of the priests and by the conditions imposed by the king, France dispatched a frigate to Hawaii in 1839 to press its demands for fair treatment of it nationals. Arriving at Honolulu that July, the captain issued an ultimatum to the government, declaring it had insulted France by "persecuting the Catholic religion, tarnishing it with the name of idolatry and expelling, under this absurd pretext, the French from this archipelago."

He made five demands: "that the Catholic worship be declared free," that the government provide a site for a Catholic church, that imprisoned Catholics be released, and that the king make a deposit of $20,000 as surety and sign such a treaty. The king had to accept these conditions. The Hawaiian constitution of 1840 provided for religious freedom in the nation.

And so, as did the kiawe tree, the Catholics spread through the islands of Hawaii. The Reverend Titus Coan had to combat them in his broad realm in Hilo and Puna on the Island of Hawaii to meet "this determined and unrelenting attack of the papal powers."

Later missionaries, however, were not so dead set against them, recognizing the obligation of tolerance instead of vindictiveness. Laura Judd admitted that the rulers had adopted "measures harsh and impolitic, which never were and never can be justified in suppressing a religious faith."

The next generation proved to be even more sympathetic and considerate. Dr. Henry Lyman remembers from his boyhood that his Hilo missionary parents considered their Catholic opponents there a "foe…dreaded more than all the rest." He recalls that, while taking a walk with his father one dusky evening, he wondered about "a strange figure" with "a shovel hat and a black frock that reached to his feet. Staring blankly through a pair of spectacles into space, it made the sign of the cross and uttered a deprecatory ejaculation as it hurried past." Henry shrank in fear when he heard it was the Roman Catholic priest, for he well knew the sad fate of martyrs under Catholic oppression.

Then Henry and his pal later "discovered a lonely native building, newly erected in an unfrequented part of town," with "a rude cross…and a few tawdry colored prints." When they learned this was the Roman Catholic chapel, he relates, "we were stricken with terror, and fled for our lives, lest we too might somehow get burned at the stake like poor John Huss, or John Rodgers and his wife with her 'nine children in arms with one at the breast'"— referring to one of the terrible tales of martyrdom he had read at home.

As he grew older, Henry "made the acquaintance of Father Charles Pougot, the refined and delicate-looking

Frenchman who cared for the parish of Hilo. I found him a very saintly seeming personage." This priest ministered to those "hardened sinners" who, "no matter how upright and virtuous their lives" otherwise, "were bundled out of the congregation" of the righteous Mr. Coan "and handed over to the tender mercies of Satan and his host." In this way, "in a short time the papal emissaries laid claim to the souls of all who were not actually enrolled on the books of the American mission," leaving Father Coan to "thunder from his pulpit against...'the mother of harlots and abominations of the earth.'"

Dr. Lyman concludes: "So these good men anathematized each other, and stood asunder as they lived. But with their antagonisms I meddled not; and when I left home for the last time, the kindly Father gave me a little French dictionary that still stands in my library. Thirty years later, when his eyesight grew dim, I sent him a mass-book, printed in the largest and clearest type that could be procured; and he responded with a cordial letter of thanks, written only a short time before his death." So the old animosities were erased by time and by the wider outlook of some in the later generations.

What would those old hard-core Calvinists of the early missionary days in Hawaii think today to learn that the Catholics are now the predominant religious group in Hawaii? They could at least find satisfaction in that these Catholics are not all converts from Protestantism but the influx of arrivals from such Catholic places as the Philippines, Portugal and Puerto Rico.

XX. EDUCATING A NATION

The development of the Hawaiian language in written form had already begun in Honolulu, according to Michener's story. Keoki and Abner discuss how the missionaries, recognizing differences of pronunciation in different places and among different people, had settled on a standard form.

"The way you Americans have decided to spell it is neither right nor wrong," Keoki admits. The true sound of his father's name, he believes, lies "between Kelolo and Teroro." Abner, defending the preference for k and l, himself trips up by pronouncing the name "Honoruru," as it was said and originally written.

When John Whipple later visits Tahiti, he notes the British rendition of their languages uses t instead of k, b in place of p, and r rather than l. So they write tabu instead of kapu. He comes to the conclusion that these are not actual differences but can be accounted for "by the difference in the ears of the men who translated them."

Abner Hale, true to missionary understanding and aims, realizes "Hawaii's greatest need: 'Teach the people to read.'" By 1828 he has three schools for Hawaiians to learn to read and write. In collaboration with other missionaries, Abner works at home at his rude desk with its whale-oil lamp translating the Bible, "his most lasting contribution to Hawaii." This is his greatest pleasure, working with Keoki and "laboring over every passage with the most minute attention."

Abner devotes himself so painstakingly to these efforts that later critics find the books he translates practically free from errors. One says in deep admiration. "It was as if he had been in turn a Hebrew and a Greek and a Hawaiian."

When Abner gets to the book of Proverbs, he happily considers it "a distillation of all the knowledge man could hope to know." But he exults with Ezekiel, as he feels these lines "spoke directly to him and epitomized his life." Was not Ezekiel "markedly similar to the prophet Abner, sitting in counsel with the alii of Maui?" Like the Hebrew prophet, Abner feels sure he can claim, "Again the word of the Lord came expressly unto me."

♠ ♠ ♠

The missionaries' first problem was to put the Hawaiian language into a visual form. So they listened and wrote down the sounds they heard to create a usable alphabet.

Their own Hawaiian alphabet, printed January 7, 1822, contained 17 letters, including b, d, r, t, and v, which they later eliminated to keep the language simplified and uniform. As Bingham explains, these letters "appeared sometimes to be interchangeable: b and p, k and t, l and r, v and w, and even the sound of d…was used in some cases where others used k, l, r, or t." Liholiho preferred the sound of "Rihoriho," though he did like the looks of his name written Liholiho.

At their General Meeting of October 21, 1825, the mission settled on a 12-letter alphabet. By that time

Bingham had already started work on a translation of Matthew, spending efforts on it daily for three weeks to complete the first chapter. He diligently compared the Latin, English, and Tahitian version with the original Greek to make the Hawaiian text "as clear and correct" as possible.

Bingham devoted 20 months to this task, collaborating with other missionaries applying their intelligence, knowledge and abilities to the art of translation. Asa Thurston at Kona, having acquired "great purity and idiomatic accuracy" in the language, with the help of Artemas Bishop and Governor Kuakini, prepared his version of the gospel. William Richards, aided by Tua, the Tahitian, and Malo, the Hawaiian, worked out another translation at Lahaina.

Meanwhile, Elias Loomis and the mission printing press were getting into action. Small leaflets for school use issued from the press first, then parts of the scriptures, and later the gospels. Back at Rochester, Loomis printed in 1828-1829 the gospels of Matthew, Mark and John, which by then had been completed. The New Testament became available to the Hawaiian people by 1832, and by 1839 the whole Bible was being printed with help from the American Bible Society.

The magic of the printed word fascinated the Hawaiians, stimulating them to eager study. The mission press flourished, turning out textbooks as more and more missionaries were contributing translations of more than 70 such books for school use. At Lahainaluna, the mission established the first school west of the Rocky Mountains in 1831, and in 1834 a second printing plant set up there helped to supply textbooks and also put out the first Hawaiian newspaper.

Within the first four years, the missionaries and their native assistants had taught one third of the people. Two years later they had schools in every district, 400 teachers, 25,000 pupils. These built up to 900 schools with 50,000 learners in the next nine years, establishing the foundation of the state school system, which the government then took over.

Besides the high school at Lahainaluna, the missionaries set up various special schools for boys and girls, as well as one for the high chiefs' children to prepare them for their future role as rulers. They also organized Punahou School for their own children so that their young ones need not be sent way off to America.

By 1840 the mission had 19 stations providing religion and education for most of the island people. Hawaii had become officially a Christian nation with "a higher per cent literacy than any contemporary country, including the homeland of the tutors."

Part Three
SPECIAL PEOPLE, SPECIAL PROBLEMS

XXI. THE MISSIONARY WHO MARRIED A HEATHEN

An agonizing scene Michener reels off is that of poor, neglected Urania Hewlett, eight months pregnant, forced to undergo a devastating journey of 40 miles over an impossible trail, the torture of which causes her son to be prematurely born and her frightful death from bleeding as Abner Hale, with the distraught husband Abraham, botches the job of the birth. During this dreadful process, the capable Hawaiian midwives lament outside, wondering why their expert aid is scorned. To the two mission aries, such a course was unthinkable, as it would be "admitting that a heathen, brown-skinned Hawaiian knew how to deliver a Christian white boy."

Left alone in an isolated outpost of this strange land and lacking the courage and confidence to carry on alone in raising his infant son, as Abner commands him, poor Abraham Hewlett resorts to the awful indiscretion of consorting with a faithful female to provide motherly care for his child. John Whipple happens by to save them from utter abomination by providing a Christian ceremony to sanctify this sinful living together.

When Abner gets this news, he is aghast that a missionary would deviate so from God's law as to live with a native woman—a heathen! Such an abhorrent thought! His former associate had gone "whoring after a heathen,"—just as the Bible warns against.

Such a falling away from missionary ethics can have but one result—condemnation and expulsion from the church by the missionary family. In response to this action, Hewlett bravely points out to them, "You love the Hawaiians as potential Christians, but you despise them as people."

When it comes to the doctor's censure for his having put religious approval on this affront to God, Whipple is more indifferent about the matter, as it is just what he expects from these associates who could tolerate no deviation from their own decisions on the will of the Lord.

♠ ♠ ♠

Michener developed this story from the experience of Mary Rice, wife of missionary William Rice. When eight months pregnant in 1841, she made her way 40 miles across the island to reach another missionary station to have her child delivered.

Alas, one missionary did fall from grace in such a manner. The American Board somehow slipped up on its requirement for only married men to go to live among the willing females of Hawaii, allowing the Reverend Samuel Gelston Dwight, graduate of Union Theological Seminary in New York, to leave with the twelfth and last company in 1847 without any wife.

From 1848 to 1854 he survived unscathed by scandal at the lonely station of Kaluaaha on "the friendly isle" of Molokai. Then he was summarily dismissed by his brother missionaries for having deserted celibacy for the comfort of a Hawaiian girl. She was one of the girl students who boarded at his house. Bradford Smith reports that lonesome Sam had been accused of indulging in the tactual pleasure of feeling a girl's tempting breasts as she sat in his lap. Then, when he found Ann Mahoe with a Hawaiian boy in her bed, he "hastily decided to marry her himself."

Smith comments, "The strange thing about it is that both Hawaiians and missionaries, after 34 years of hearing and preaching the doctrine of Christian love, still regarded the marriage of a missionary with a Hawaiian girl as degrading to him." Smith then quotes the scornful question of missionary Judd's son Charles: "Do you think I would marry a girl with native blood?—far from it." And Smith adds, "The mission children did not share Charlie Judd's prejudice, for six mission families in the second generation married Hawaiians...In the next generation after Charlie, the Judd family also intermarried."

As for Samuel Dwight, the only missionary to enjoy Hawaiian matrimony, his life was blessed with seven children. To four of them he gave as middle names the surnames of other missionaries whom he had admired and loved. Sam and Anna died within a few months of each other some 25 years after their union. Samuel Dwight did not desert the Christian religion after its Hawaiian authorities had banned him. He stayed on at Kaluaaha to serve as scribe until 1857 and operated a dairy there. Then, in Honolulu during his last years, he was supporting the Fort Street Church, being especially active in its Sunday School.

♠ ♠ ♠

At the tragic death of Urania Hewlett, Michener comments that she was "the first of many mission women to die in childbirth or from physical exhaustion due to overwork."

Records show that 11 out of the 75 wives did succumb within the first ten years of struggle under missionary conditions in Hawaii. Mrs. Mary Ward Rogers died of childbirth the first year after her marriage to Edmund Rogers, having served in Hawaii five years before that. Another lost life after the birth of her second child in three years after arrival. Two held out for four years, two more for five years, three for six years, and one each for eight and ten years.

These early victims produced in their brief lives 27 children, six of them bearing two children and two each with three and four children. The other 64 wives held good records of longevity.

The first adult death in the mission was that of Elizabeth, wife of Artemas Bishop, at Kailua in 1828, five years after her arrival and the birth of two children.

XXII. THE WAYWARD PUPIL

Abner starts his school for Hawaiian girls, and Pupali enrolls his four lovely daughters whose visits aboard whaling ships had brought him so much profit. Iliki, the youngest, prettiest and most enticing, starts school first and soon becomes Jerusha's ablest pupil, and "her greatest joy was [this] young Iliki, who had once run off to the whalers but who could now recite the Psalms." And "run off to the whalers" is just what Iliki and her three sisters are doing in the book nine pages later. Jerusha closes her school for that day as she sees "that the mission's moral teaching had been outraged."

Iliki's sisters then "became the dancers at Murphy's grog shop," but she "was allowed to stay in the mission school, and under Jerusha's most careful guidance grew to understand the Bible and to forswear whaling ships." Jerusha enjoys visions of lovely Iliki married to some Christian Hawaiian and becoming "the best wife in the islands." Abner too is counting on just such a happy ending, with his performing the wedding ceremony.

But Michener's evil plot is to hold no such felicitous arrangement for this "bright-eyed beauty," who again leaps up from school and dashes "madly away" to the familiar whaleship to become the prize of Abner's hateful rival, Captain Hoxworth, who, in turn, later gives the much-desired Iliki to an English ship captain. All this causes much despair for the Hales, as their fond hopes for Iliki are so cruelly crushed. Abner's "love for the child Iliki" haunts his memories, and, as he becomes "an increasingly befuddled man," he keeps seeking news of her fate from every new ship that arrives in Lahaina.

♠ ♠ ♠

One promising mission student named Leoiki did have a similar experience. She was the Hawaiian girl whom the whaling ship captain had purchased from a female chief for $160. It was this captain's men who attacked the home of William Richards when they found that such free opportunities for female procurement were denied them on their next visit to Lahaina.

But the more important and prominent case of a valued student's defection from mission supervision was not that of a native girl but of one who was a *hapahaole* (half white), the delightful combination of American breeding plus the gayety and sensitiveness of the Hawaiian. This is the story of Hannah Holmes.

Hannah possessed some of the New England scholarly interest of the respected Holmes family of Plymouth, Massachusetts, as well as some of the glamor of the Hawaiian alii. Her father, Oliver Holmes, arriving at Honolulu as a sailor in 1793, decided his prospects were more attractive in Hawaii than on the sea.

He proudly kept the discharge paper his captain granted him, attesting that Holmes "ever behaved with great propriety, as an honest and active man."

Holmes won favor with King Kamehameha, married Mahi, a Hawaiian chiefess, gained grants of land on Oahu and Molokai, built up a fine private establishment in Honolulu with houses for his expanding family, for his 180 tenants, and for entertaining visiting captains. With profit from his estates, trade, and services to ship captains, he could live in native luxury, his thatched houses graced with the best of goods from America and China. In time he became one of the four leading foreign assistants to Kamehameha and one of the most important men in the kingdom and governor of Oahu.

His family grew as he and Mahi produced "a houseful of buxom, fun loving girls who combined the soft, languorous Hawaiian qualities with a western vivacity and forwardness that visiting seamen found irresistible," according to Bradford Smith's lively account. Polly at 14 was carried off on a cruise by a ship captain and became a young mother.

Ship captains naturally sought to relieve their rather dreary lives with female companionship. So it was that Captain William Heath Davis, an earlier active leader in Pacific trade and one who helped establish the sandalwood market in 1811, while enjoying life as a guest in the Holmes household, developed a fond fascination for Oliver's alluring 16-year-old j daughter Hannah. The next year (1817) he married her, which, in Hawaii at that time, meant that he set up a conjugal relationship with her. They celebrated the event by setting off on a nuptial cruise to California. Their first son, Robert Grimes Davis, was born in 1819.

Captain Davis, a garrulous social and political leader of the local traders, had profusely welcomed the missionaries and volunteered to help supply their needs. And that he did when Daniel Chamberlain needed a pump for his well. Davis got him one from an old ship rotting in the harbor. As he worked, he tried to explain to the mission men the natural need of the seafaring gentry for native wives, either permanent or temporary.

When Sybil Bingham opened her day school in that first year of the mission, Hannah Holmes (she always kept her maiden name) became one of her star pupils. Hannah did have some advantage at the start, as, having had an American father and an American husband, she could understand English. She progressed rapidly in her studies and eagerly devoted herself to Bible reading and prayer.

With Hannah, four other Holmes children graced the humble missionary school, as she was accompanied by her younger sisters, Mary, Polly, Jennie and Charlotte, and her brother George, all of whom shone splendidly as promising scholars and made their father proud when he witnessed their accomplishments at the school's first public examination.

Hannah invited the Binghams to her sumptuous home to conduct Sabbath evening prayer meetings. Friends and neighbors were happy to join in on these occasions hosted by the charming Hannah. As Bingham read from the lamp-illuminated Bible, Hannah sat at his feet and told the others in Hawaiian what he was reading and saying in English. They held prayers, sang a hymn, and old Oliver Holmes shed some tears as he heard once more the familiar music and words of the sacred hymns he had sung in his youthful church-going days at home in Massachusetts.

The mission was so happy to have such a radiant, devoted girl as Hannah as a leading scholar. She was blessed by her father with "her love of order, propriety, decorum and a brooding sense of duty that turned easily to one of guilt," as Albertine Loomis judges her character. So it puzzled the mission when Hannah stopped coming to school and services. Then it was that they finally learned the facts of Hannah's life—that she was living with Captain Davis, had borne him a son and was about to present him with another child.

Hannah's growing adherence to the strict religious demands of Bingham influenced Davis to withdraw her from such views antagonistic to his own liberal outlook. A gregarious fellow, he still sought the company of the missionary families, but, often deep in his cups, he began to growl more about their affairs and attitudes. Bingham went to talk with Davis and, in his forceful, direct way, managed to soothe the captain's spirit enough so that, soon after, Captain Davis took a bolt of cloth as a present to the mission and was accepted as a guest and joined the family at tea. But he ignored Bingham's request that Hannah be allowed to return to school.

Down in his heart, the captain was still perturbed by fear of the mission's invading his private life and turning Hannah away from him. Resentment continued to fester in his heart until he came out in open warfare against the mission. He felt more and more strongly that these high-minded missionaries were wrecking his Pacific paradise by undermining the love and faithfulness of his dear Hannah.

For Hannah had been acquiring fresh values of mind, manners and morals. She was unhappy being kept at home away from the mission. Elisha and Maria Loomis visited her one day when Davis was not at home. They reported that "Hannah had received them eagerly, asked about everyone at the mission, invited them to try out the splendid hand organ the captain had lately bought, clung to Maria's hand and wept a little when they left."

In his bitterness at the changes in Hannah's attitude, Davis threatened the withdrawal of all the Holmes children. But Oliver Holmes held the mission in greater respect. He kept four of his children as day pupils, while Charlotte remained as a boarding student. Even when the high-born Mahi took Charlotte away from the school because her daughter had been scolded, Oliver ushered the girl right back to the New England discipline, which he felt she should learn to respect.

When Oliver's wife died after the birth of her next child, the mission adopted George and the baby. Oliver Holmes gratefully appreciated the sincere efforts of the missionaries even though he did feel too that they in some ways interfered with his life and that of his family. These were puzzling times with such conflicting customs to deal with.

Great changes came into Hannah's life in 1822. She produced William Heath Davis, Jr., the elder Davis finally drank himself to death, and John Coffin Jones, the recently arrived trader and first American consul in Hawaii, manfully took over Davis's marital obligations. Hannah was a choice object of male interest that Jones was happy to acquire. Jones had conducted Davis's funeral to the approval of "more than 3,000 souls present," according to Marin's diary. But Marin added, "All the American gentlemen were disgusted with the sermon of the missionaries."

As consul, Jones administered the estate of Captain Davis and soon took Hannah and her two young sons into his home. He proved to be a good stepfather to the boys. He sent Robert to Boston to live with Jones's wealthy uncle and "receive a classical education." His younger stepson, William Heath Davis, Jr., he took with him as cabin boy on two voyages to California, when the lad was 9 and 11, then entered him in the new Oahu Charity School.

After Jones sailed back to Boston on business in 1824, Hannah remained at home for months, then, her religious interests rekindled, she returned to the mission to school and church services. The missionaries rejoiced at her reaffirmation of Christian principles and grew confident that nothing now could tear her away from them.

Her father also died while Jones was away. Like his friend Captain Davis, he succumbed to hearty imbibing of liquor. His funeral was a big affair, attended by his numerous bibulous friends. And, in his honor, regretting the loss of a faithful customer, the grog shops lowered their flags to half mast. Though quite out of step with such people and the demonstrations, a couple missionaries did feel inclined to pay their respects to Hannah's father by joining the procession, until they found they were among men gayly flaunting their companionship with Holmes's less restrained daughters as well as with more notorious mistresses and prostitutes.

Holmes's friends spurned the thought of having Bingham preach the funeral sermon. As Charles Stewart happened to be in Honolulu at the time, they did have him offer a prayer for the departed friend.

Hannah's stability in the mission met a fresh crisis. John Coffin Jones had returned. He sought to renew his relationship with Hannah, but now strong in her renewed faith, she refused to live with him without a marriage blessed by the church. Any favorable feelings he may have held toward the mission vanished then, and he raged in bitterness against this "religion...crammed down the throats of these poor simple mortals" and accused his

Yankee preacher associates with being "infamous, degrading, revolting...trampling on men's rights on the pretense of saving souls."

Jones realized he had good reason to feel discriminated against, as getting settled in holy matrimony was not at all the local custom up to that time. You just "took" a Hawaiian wife—maybe more than one—and lived with her as long as was convenient. But Jones did not just fume over the affair. He was a charming gentleman who knew how to handle women.

Hannah did try to stay away from him. One report claims she intended to go to Maui with William Richards to stay with Kaahumanu, who had taken an active interest in her. But Loomis says, "She was not that much of a Puritan" to run away from love. Jones's biographer expresses the view that she did go and Jones followed her there. As Gast explains, "Apparently she could not resist the suit of the handsome and persuasive young Bostonian, for by the end of the year (1826) they were living together again."

Gentleman Jones respected and loved Hannah in his own selfish way and so worked things gradually and with inducements. As the Holmes thatched houses were now in bad condition, Jones replaced them with a fine, large mansion of coral block as Hannah's personal domain. Before long, Hannah was with Jones at his country seat, but she too was bothered by the dilemma of life—love man or love God? Or how to make the two compatible?

Such wavering must have affected Jones' relationship with her. Daws writes that she "alternately shared Jones' bed and deserted him for Christ. "So Jones added to his feminine interests Lahilahi Marin, the 16–year-old daughter of another prominent foreign adviser to Kamehameha I, Don Francisco de Paula Marin, and owner of an estate next to that of Oliver Holmes. Jones knew how to pick them. Gast refers to Lahilahi as "a very attractive young woman, with the vivacity of her Andalusian forebears and the dusky beauty of her mother's race. Earlier the Prince Kauikeaouli had indicated he would like her as his future queen. The American gentleman again proved himself the persuasive one.

Jones' dual menage began to produce results. Hannah presented him with a daughter Elizabeth in 1830, and Lahilahi gave him a son Francis. In 1832 Lahilahi had a daughter Rosalie.

Jones was a very active man in other respects. His duties as American consul by no means prevented his being involved in his work as agent for an influential Boston firm and serving his personal ambitions by engaging in his own trading schemes. By 1836 his enterprises took him a second time to California to confer with his partner in Santa Barbara. At a big "fandango" put on at his partner's villa, Jones feasted his eyes and desires on the charming young sister of his partner's wife. Manuela Carillo, like his feminine conquests in Hawaii, was a tempting young miss, age 17, just ripe for inspiring fond dreams in the mind of her 40-year-old admirer.

While Jones was on his return voyage to Honolulu, Lahilahi was giving birth to his second son, whom he honored with the name John Coffin Jones III.

A man of Jones' prominence naturally took an active part in social affairs and politics. All this won him many friends and likewise a due number of enemies. After his joining in the "epistolary war" of 1837 over the rejection of the returned Catholic priests, his opponents—sea captains, mission aries, the king and chiefs—petitioned the American president to replace him.

Unaware of all these forces working against him, Jones later that year returned to Santa Barbara for a stay of 18 months. He got baptized by a Catholic priest and in June, 1838, married his fiancee, then 18 when he was 42. This time there was no question of avoiding a legal church marriage.

While there, he wrote to his stepson, Hannah's William Heath Davis, Jr., trusting he was on good behavior at school, promising to send him a horse, and persuading him to "look after little Johnny and Elizabeth and his mother." But William, then age 16, made his own plans. He too set off for California the very month that Jones was married. In San Francisco he went to work with his uncle, who had married his mother's sister, Jane Holmes. In time he won and lost a fortune but established his reputation as a California historian.

Six months after his marriage, Jones rashly took his bride to his lair in Honolulu. Jones' friends honored the returning consul and his new wife with several parties. In the course of events it became clear that Manuela "was not the stereotyped, sheltered, convent-reared Spanish senorita, but very worldly for an 18-year-old." This was well for her under the circumstances of her husband's marital entanglements.

Hannah naturally objected to the situation. After all, Jones had refused to give her a Christian wedding. She complained to the regent, who summoned Jones and, after his refusals, prompted his appearance by threatening to have him forcibly dragged in. Self-assured, he refused to give up Manuela, as ordered, and return to Hannah while in Hawaii. The king then advised him that he was guilty of the crime of bigamy, had treated his government with contempt, and therefore could no longer be recognized as consul. None of them knew that Jones' letter of dismissal had already been on its way from the United States for several months.

Hannah and Lahilahi together came for a long talk with their former lover. It seems that he agreed to property settlements with them, as later Hannah was granted his country home and Lahilahi kept the one that he had built for her.

Jones' popularity in Honolulu sparked a gathering of 60 of his friends and well-wishers at a farewell dinner for him when he left for Santa Barbara early in 1840.

The occasion went down in history as "the largest gathering of local residents ever assembled at one table in Honolulu" up to that time. Had there been room, more than a hundred would have been on hand to voice their praise of the departing consul. Jones' ten-minute address "touched lovingly on passing events" during his career there, bringing "deafening cheers" from his admirers. The report was that sponsors spent more than $3000 on this affair.

Hannah, who had led such an unstable existence as Jones' supposed wife, was by no means pining away for any lost love. As the beautiful daughter of a former governor of Oahu, living in one of the most pretentious houses in Honolulu, Hannah took an active part in the social life of the city. Late in that year that Jones left, she appeared as the charming hostess entertaining 200 guests in honor of 60 officers of the American exploring expedition under Commodore Wilkes. The spacious living room of her large coral mansion displayed the flags of many nations. A bountiful array of food and beautiful island belles provided elements for a gay social evening, attended by the governor and climaxed by a hearty round of toasts.

For a time, Hannah used her grand home for a dancing school, directed by Stephen Reynolds, a friend and associate of Jones. Reynolds played the fiddle and aimed to teach the young daughters of white men the social graces he felt they should have for polite society. But the reputation enjoyed by Hannah and her girl friends was such that "proper ladies" would refrain from inviting them into their parlors.

Hannah's connection with the missionary families was by then entirely broken off, and they readily expressed their disapproval of the kind of life she was leading. They openly criticized her and her daughter Elizabeth, who, at 13, was already quite advanced and experienced for her age, deploring their conduct, dress, and the probable source of their fine clothing.

Jones made three more visits to Honolulu each year from 1842 to 1844, showing special interest in his maturing daughter Elizabeth. Each time he conducted her to dancing classes, later held at Reynolds' coral home. On his first trip he brought her a saddle mare and a new dress. Hannah quite determinedly refused his request to take Elizabeth to California with him. He expressed his appreciation to Reynolds for the consideration he had shown his daughter and urged him to continue to look after her. On his final visit, Jones again spent much of his time with Elizabeth. No record appears of any visit to Hannah or to Lahilahi and her children, though Lahilahi may not have been there then, as she died sometime that year.

Jones learned of Hannah's death in 1847 from her son Robert. In response, Jones expressed his regrets that because of his misfortunes he could not provide for his daughter, who was then 17, and asked Davis to take care of her and protect her. Her half brother knew only too well how she was taking care of herself. The next year she married J. H. Brown and died in 1852 at the age of 22. She had no children.

Jones' daughter Rosalie married Richard Gilliland in 1854 and had five children. Only through her was Jones' blood line passed on in Hawaii. Her brother Francis had died unmarried in 1850, and John Coffin died in 1865 without leaving any children.

It was Hannah's second son, Robert Grimes Davis, who helped continue her blood line. After getting his education in Boston between 1825 and 1841, he returned to Hawaii, practiced law, and later served in the courts of the kingdom and as associate justice in the reign of Kamehameha V. He married Harriet Hammet, a cousin, and their daughter, Charlotte Holmes Davis, married a Captain James Anderson King. Their son, Samuel Wilder King, as the eleventh governor in the territorial government of 1953-1957, became the first one with Hawaiian blood that of his great great grandmother Mahi. The governor's son, Samuel P. King, born in China in 1916, when his father commanded a U.S. gunboat on the Yangtze River, serves as federal judge in Hawaii.

Unhappy with his state of affairs in California, Jones took his family to Boston in 1846. Dissatisfaction and ill health plagued him until he died near the end of 1861. He left his wife, Manuela, and six children, four of them born in Massachusetts. She remarried, her new husband being George F. Kettle, a widower with three children.

XXIII. The Queen Leads The Way To Christ

Michener creates Malama as the one high chiefess with which Abner has to deal and makes her the usually fatty kind—or, in one of Bingham's phrases, one of "unseemly obesity." She had been the 19th wife in Kamehameha's collection of 21. Her husband Kelolo is also her brother, a dual relationship vociferously condemned by Abner. He spends much time and effort to drive into her heart the intense fear that she would "die in hellfire" and suffer "the fire forever" with incessant "pain...horrible beyond imagining."

Kelolo must go, Abner commands. Though Malama half-heartedly consents, her love for her partner is so great that she can not renounce entirely her relationship with him or her sacred connections with the Hawaiian spirits.

Malama is so quick in her studies that Jerusha marvels at her speed. Learning to see the evils about her as Abner points them out so feelingly, she accepts his religious pronouncements and makes moral reforms. As she is, in Abner's eyes, "rapidly approaching a state of grace," her health begins to fail. Now she fears the end and suffers the torment of her soul lest she be denied access to the Christian heaven. "I am going to die and I want to speak to God before I do," she beseeches Abner.

Abner yields to her entreaties and agrees to baptize her on Sunday. That will be too late, Dr. Whipple believes. They baptize her and she receives a Christian burial. But, still clinging to her life-long faith in Hawaiian gods, she has arranged with Kelolo for her old-time kahunas to add native rites after her burial.

♠ ♠ ♠

The story of Queen Keopuolani is the source of much of this story. The big difference from Malama is in her size. She was not one of those "heavy, corpulent persons" like most of the other queens. Her outstanding ancestry had placed her in the highest position at that time among the wives of Kamehameha the Great. She was the queen-mother of Liholiho, then ruling as Kamehameha II, of little Kauikeaouli, destined to become Kamehameha III, and of his younger sister Princess Nahienaena. Stewart translates Keopuolani as meaning "The Gathering of the Heavens."

It was she who first broke away from the native religion, before the missionaries arrived, by eating with her young son Kauikeaouli in defiance of that tabu. Later she induced the young king to make this break in the tabu official by seating himself at the women's table at a feast. On seeing him perform this daring act of defiance to the gods, "The guests, astonished at this act, clapped their hands cried out, "Ai noa,—the eating tabu is broken,'" according to the report of Kaahumanu, the other conspiring queen and regent with Liholiho. That set the stage for the next blows against the religion the destruction of the heiaus (temples) and the burning of the wooden idols sacred to the gods.

As a pleasant escape from the dreary scene of Honolulu, the chiefs enjoyed Waikiki, "an out station" a few miles east of the city, "for its extensive groves of cocoanut and kou trees." In the spring of 1823 Keopuolani, "in feeble health," "pitched her tent, and sojourned (there) for a time." Bingham rejoiced then at seeing the highest chief "attend to the things spoken to her from the Scriptures" and express her desire that these "be repeated from Sabbath to Sabbath."

With great satisfaction, Bingham contrasted her state of grace with her, "heathen state" 16 years before, when she was also ill and Kamehameha had had ten men seized to be sacrificed to appease the gods and prevent her death. Luckily she had recovered in time for seven of the doomed men to be released. "Her life was spared," Bingham explains, "to see that period of gross darkness, malevolence, and blood, pass away; and to hear of the sacrifice of Christ offered once for all. She reproved the wickedness of some of the 'dark hearted' chiefs around her" and declared "I will never return to that evil course—I fear the everlasting fire." Bingham had done this persuasion well.

And so Keopuolani sought to do everything righteous and "obey Christ." She agreed "it was wrong to have two husbands" and conceded, "I desire but one. Hoapili is my husband; hereafter my only husband." With that, she sent away her other husband.

In Keopuolani, Bingham had made his grandest conquest in his cause of Christianizing the nation. "She rejoiced that the knowledge of the great salvation had been brought to the land...but exclaimed, 'Lamentable that the true religion did not reach us in our childhood!'" As Bingham understood Hawaiian history, she had "spent more than half a gloomy century in the darkness, pollution, and cruelties of heathenism." "Her conversion to the gospel," he felt was "a forcible appeal...to Christian sympathy to hasten the work of evangelization."

Keopuolani also made pleasing progress in mastering the new art of reading. Stewart was pleased to note, "Keopuolani is indefatigable in her efforts to learn to read in her own tongue." The missionaries had instilled in her the determined desire to learn "enough of the good word [of God] and of the right way to go to heaven." With such ambition, she had, Stewart witnessed, freed herself "from all the reproaches of heathenism" and appeared "sincerely desirous of fully imbibing the spirit, as well as observing the forms, of Christianity."

Though she was only 45, Stewart refers to her as "being aged," as she was suffering in ill health and fear of dying before her religious training was sufficient to provide her with her longed-for pathway to heaven.

Early in September, 1823, Keopuolani became so seriously ill that a man came to warn the missionaries she was already dead. They hurried to her but "found that she was only more ill and would soon die." Her religious spirit dominated her. "Great indeed is my love for God!" she assured the assembled chiefs. "She was too feeble to say more," Stewart realized, "but seemed in a state of mind to give much stronger testimony to the excellency and power, even in death, of the religion we had brought her."

It was a week later that Stewart found "the dying hour of our kind patroness and friend...fast approaching." The night previous he and Dr. Abraham Blatchley, the missionary physician summoned from Honolulu, had found her "very ill." Auna, a Tahitian chief, had, at her request for "the good word," talked with her for half an hour about religion and "concluded with a most spiritual and fervent prayer."

Now her son Liholiho, the king, and Kaahumanu and Kalanimoku, were urging the missionaries to let her be baptized, as she had begged "to be washed with water, in the name of God." The king gave their reasons: "because she was a Christian, had the true faith in her heart, had given herself to Jesus Christ long before she was sick, and because all the people of God were baptized, and she had herself so earnestly requested it."

Then came the report, "The queen is dead!" The whole heavens rung with lamentations and woe, and the natives were fleeing with their meager possessions to avoid the terrible consequences of "all kinds of extravagance, violence, and abomination" that regularly occurred at times of mourning. But William Ellis soon came dashing back with the reassurance that Keopuolani had only fainted and had revived. Since her "fluttering spirit" could not be roused, Ellis "proceeded at length to administer the sacred ordinance" to award her "the name of Christian." And the missionaries prayed for her immortal soul to speed to "the house of God and the gate of heaven."

"Thus," Stewart concludes, "the highest chief of the Sandwich Islands, after having given satisfactory evidence of a renewed heart, and of sincere love to Jesus Christ, was initiated into the visible church of God: and as we hope and believe, in the course of an hour after, joined the invisible church above, having triumphed over the power of death and the grave."

The fears of extreme violence proved to be groundless. Keopuolani had "long before," according to Kalanimoku, the prime minister, "forbidden every heathen practice at her death." Two days later, Keopuolani was laid to rest in "the first Christian funeral of a high chief that has ever taken place in the islands." Stewart could rest assured that "she calmly awaits the resurrection in the decent habiliments of a Christian tomb."

XXIV. The Royal Dilemma—Hawaii Or Heaven?

An explosive setback that sends Abner raging in a wild dramatic scene is the frightful "abomination" of the mating of brother and sister contrary to the laws of God. Overcome by disbelief, Abner mumbles that "They can't go back to Kane!…They're Congregationalists!" Then Abner flies into a fury of denunciation, strikes down "the sacred stone of Kane," has to be dragged away, and succumbs to hysterical laughter at "the hideousness of this night,—the hulas, the living stone, the drums and the kahunas."

Abner is completely baffled by such drastic change in events. Jerusha stops his ranting by making the honest judgment that he is "making a fool" of himself and points out that they "are here engaged in a tremendous battle 'between the old gods and the new.'" Then, seeing Abner is hurt by her unorthodox terminology, she changes it to "between heathenish ways and the ways of the Lord."

♠ ♠ ♠

The Hawaiians were struggling to find ways to cope with the profound changes in their lives. A strange, new religion was being thrust upon the nation, leaving many minds floundering between long-time native beliefs, attitudes and customs and the new powers of restraint and different aims. Still fond of their normal and natural ways of life, yet attracted by the great truths the missionaries offered them, Hawaiians wavered between the two extremes of culture.

In striking evidence of this popular perplexity was the tragic story of a royal brother and sister struggling to find their way between their inherited powers and high position and the imported requirements of a religious faith imposing new demands on them.

As Keopuolani ranked highest among all the chiefs of Hawaii, her three children by Kamehameha the Great naturally stood above all others in the Hawaiian kingdom. The oldest, Liholiho, ruled as Kamehameha II. Next in line came Prince Kauikeaouli and his sister Princess Nahienaena.

Born to rule, they had to be treated by all with great honor, respect and homage. In 1823 when Charles Stewart came first to know the prince and princess, they dwelt in separate houses taken care of by a large staff of attendants and were "left very much to their own will" in spite of guardians and nurses. With such freedom, they lived much like the youthful example Stewart observed on the streets of Honolulu, "under no control but his own will, and enjoyed already the privileges of his birth, in...doing whatever he pleased."

Brought up thus in luxury and power, the young prince and princess came to feel their own importance and enjoy the deference of those about them. As less than two years separated them in age, they were often together and came to feel a close relationship. They enjoyed the pomp and power of court affairs and their prominence among the important people about them in carrying on native traditions. But they lived in those disrupting days when the good and the bad of the white man's ways increasingly caused confusion in the uncertain course of the nation.

Nahienaena's name meant "hot fires" and those fires in her spirit faltered and flared according to circumstances and her moods, as she swayed from one direction to the other. Descended from gods in a centuries-old culture that had reached its zenith under her father, King

Kamehameha the Great, she became faced with the problem of adapting to the revolutionary civilization divided between reckless, greedy adventurers and the stern, demanding missionaries.

Impressively she appears first in missionary annals as Bingham describes her part in Liholiho's 1823 celebration of his becoming king. Up to his palace she rides "in a four-wheeled carriage fantastically decorated, and drawn by her friends and servants." She was 8 years old then. The king lifts her up on his back to carry her to the table and seats her "by the side of Kauikeaouli, the young prince, with whom she held equal rank."

Just a few days later Stewart reached Honolulu with the second company of missionaries and saw Nahienaena brought to the welcoming function at the palace on a man's shoulders and followed by a train of 20 or 30 boys and girls. She was dressed in European fashion "in black satin trimmed with broad gold lace, with black satin hat and feathers." Stewart observed, "She is a very pretty and well-behaved child, [even] to our own ideas of the characteristics of childhood."

It was destined that Stewart and his partner, William Richards, would become the overseers of Nahienaena's fate. At the request of her mother, suffering, as she had much of her life, from ill health, they all removed from dusty, busy Honolulu to the more pleasant and peaceful port of Lahaina on Maui. There the two new arrivals established their mission with

Keopuolani's help, thus providing care and Christian direction for her and her husband, Hoapili, and Nahienaena. There the dowager queen became the first Christian convert, baptized just before her death.

One of her parting wishes, Bingham says she expressed, was "her earnest desire that...the prince and the princess, then able to read and write, might be well educated, and particularly that Nahienaena might be trained up in the habits of Christian and civilized females, like the wives of the missionaries." Thus a haughty young chiefess who had savored pomp and favoritism was destined to bow to the rules and regulations of a new religion. Though the chiefs still ruled and carried on their native customs, she became subject to the influence of a new source of power in the changing world about her.

Bingham did understand the dangers and stresses with which the young princess would have to contend. She was "an interesting pupil," he wrote, "though in her childhood and surrounded with heathen pollution." The missionary group wished to protect her from corruption by keeping her with them, but Bingham had to admit "this could be accomplished only in part" because of her attachment to her high position and her duty to the Hawaiian people. The religious rule to which she was subjected was, in Bingham's own words, one "that holds no compromise with the vile pleasures and criminal indulgences of those who love darkness rather than light."

Though the missionaries maintained this educational and moral supremacy over the princess, she had to lead a dual life. As a royal person taking part in court affairs, she lived on a far grander scale, acting the part for which she was born. Even at church services she appeared in royal splendor, attired in rich European style and attended by her standard bearer and maids of honor.

According to Hawaiian tradition, Nahienaena had a sacred part to play in preserving the royal supremacy. Brother-sister marriages had played an essential role in perpetuating the divine succession of kings and queens. Her mother's high rank derived from her royal blood as the child of a half-brother and -sister union. Recognizing the advantages of such a marriage in this case, the chiefs talked with Elisha Loomis, missionary printer and teacher, on such a prospect. His predictable response was that it would be absolutely immoral—incest prohibited by the Bible and by all civilized peoples.

But what else could they do? No prospective partners of the right rank and age for the prince and the princess could be found. This royal marriage could be the only natural, logical solution to this problem of state. It was also quite natural for the boy and girl involved, who had enjoyed a fond companionship during childhood. And Loomis unhappily admitted that such incest seemed to exist already in this case, as, he declared, people openly talked of the prince and princess sleeping together.

Nahienaena restlessly progressed, fluctuating between the grandeur of court life and her groping for salvation. The royal pair commemorated the death of their mother by putting on a grand pageant, in which Nahienaena dazzled the admiring multitudes by appearing in a succession of splendid robes, each time accompanied by fresh groups of attendants. The ensuing banquet ended in a scene of wild drunkenness.

Then, aroused by fears she was beset by a sorcerer's spells, she went off with a native priest to sacrifice to the old gods. Rebounding from this offense to the Jehovah she had accepted, she became again a devout Christian. At a women's church meeting she led the congregation in prayers.

More temptations came her way. What girl's mind could not be ravished by the magnificence of a skirt, nine yards long, made from the rare yellow bird feathers? Her faithful followers in Lahaina worked a long time to fashion this for her. To Richards, who had just impressed on her the need for modesty and humility, she confessed her fear of such a grand garment, regretfully admitting, "It is a thing to lift up one's heart."

Yet she was indeed to present herself in such extravagant finery, though not, as intended, for her welcoming of her older brother, Kamehameha II, who had gone off to London on a visit. It was at a formal reception for the officers of the frigate *Blonde*, which brought back the bodies of the dead king and queen, that Nahienaena could splendidly display her pretentious skirt of yellow feathers, as Stewart observed, lined with crimson satin. Yet she was pleasingly modest. In her spirit of grace, she had refused to don it as a native costume because she would have had to appear naked to the waist with only wreaths for her head and neck. The precious skirt had to be "thrown carelessly about her over her European dress." Stewart applauded her spirit and restraint.

Nahienaena continued to put aside elements of pride and pleasure as she faithfully followed her Christian teachings. Aiming to emulate the lofty example of Kaahumanu and Kalanimoku, who became church members late in 1825, she devoted herself to such an exemplary religious existence as to be accepted by the church, having fulfilled its strict requirements for membership by her sound standing as a "child of God" with "stability of Christian character."

Well aware of the political and religious advantages of such an important event, the missionaries staged this spiritual recognition of a princess in January, 1827, when Kalanimoku stopped at Lahaina. Then Nahienaena and a high chiefess, along with several others, were baptized "in the presence of a vast concourse of people; and the Lord's Supper was administered," Bingham proudly put down in his record.

Her spiritual progress continued to please Bingham as he remarked with satisfaction that, while she was in Honolulu later that year, being "supposed to be seriously seeking, not only to secure the salvation of her own soul, but to know how she might honor God and do good to the people in her high station," she refused to play cards when invited to tea at the home of a British resident.

But bad rumors of the conduct of the brother, now king, and his sister continued to circulate. She loved her brother and enjoyed the greater freedom away from the direct control of the missionary family. The young king, having been brought up without such domination over his spirit, lived a merry life usually free from religious restraint. In this busy city, temptations abounded. Even in Lahaina, life was brighter and gayer a few months later, when the king visited there.

Yet, dissolute though the king was considered, he could still impressively play the part of a monarch advising his subjects to respect the new religion and revere God. He performed nobly at the dedication of the fourth church building in Honolulu on July 3, 1829. With some 4,000 people assembled, "the king, in his Windsor uniform, and his sister, in a dress becoming her high rank and improved character and taste," played their parts perfectly.

The king addressed the attentive assemblage "in a handsome appropriate manner," proclaiming, "Chiefs, teachers, and commons, hear: we have assembled here to dedicate to Jehovah, my God, this house of prayer which I have built for him. Here let us worship him, listen to the voice of his ministers, and obey his words." He then lent his good bass voice and the princess her good treble to the choir's rendition of the hundredth psalm.

When Charles Stewart, who had left the islands in 1825 because of his wife's continued illness, returned as navy chaplain on the USS *Vincennes* in October, 1829, he soon became distressed at the continued accusations that the young royal pair had lived together "in a state of licentiousness and incest." Hastening to Lahaina, he confronted Nahienaena with these evil reports. She went into a state of depression. Impressed by her sincere sorrow and her denials, Stewart became convinced that such "incrimination was as false in fact, as it was heinous in its nature." The chiefs likewise strongly refuted such evil charges, asserting they were a "false and lying report."

Nahienaena wrote a letter to Mrs. Stewart, whom she had loved and admired, and after whom she had taken the name Harriet, as had her mother also. In it she expressed her troublesome problem. She lived in two conflicting worlds with far different standards of what was proper or condemned. She earnestly sought the kingdom of God, but her thoughts became "ensnared: and thus it is continually," she lamented. She felt doomed in her dilemma.

Irreconcilable Cultures

Back in Lahaina, Nahienaena, after the prominent part she had played in the pageant presented before the officers of the *Vincennes*, faced the difficulty of settling down to good behavior. Among the Hawaiian royalty in Honolulu at the celebration, she had held the center of attraction, seated on a high platform, brilliant in her splendid yellow feather skirt over her black satin gown and, over her shoulders, a yellow feather cloak accented with red and black designs. In response to Captain Finch's bowing to her, she had removed the cloak and had a young chief take it to the captain. When the royal party left in procession, Stewart waxed eloquent in his admiration for "the animated and youthful favorite passing triumphantly along" and "surrounded by all the glory of her rank and the gaze of ten thousand eyes...the joy of the people and the delight of the whole nation."

What a comedown from such a glorious triumph to the drab life in Lahaina. Seeking some amusement, she resorted to playing cards, drinking wine and listening to ancient chants, much to the annoyance of the missionaries. She manifested more disrespect for them by disturbing Sunday church services with her late arrival accompanied by her retinue. Her restlessness seemed to reflect the eruption of lawlessness among the people, following the bad example of their king. He roved recklessly about, abandoning himself to the proverbial personal pleasures of wine, women and song.

Nahienaena made another turn-about. A feeling of remorse at her faithlessness sent her seeking protection from her failings by going to live in the Richards family home. There she remained steadfast for a year. Then she yielded again to drink, confessed her bad conduct, suffered suspension from church communion, then, reinstated, was back on her good behavior under Richards' control.

Kaahumanu died in Honolulu on June 5, 1832, attended by the king princess and chiefs. At her funeral, a new missionary observed, "The young Princess Harriet...appeared truly dignified and composed. There was something in her countenance that told a tenderness of feeling and a firmness of soul."

Freed from the restraining influence of the regent, the king reveled in enjoying his own way. He revived ancient customs and deviated into wild extravagances of conduct, such as ordering a mock court of prostitutes to pay tribute to his mistress.

After debating for a month over what could be done with this recalcitrant monarch, the chiefs decided to try to get him away from his rowdy gang to their supervision in Lahaina. Nahienaena was brought to Honolulu to persuade her brother. He consented, and brother and sister strolled hand in hand to the wharf to depart. But, on the way, he left her to stop to visit a friend and never reappeared, leaving her alone "weeping and wailing for her brother."

Considering events a little later and weighing the wins and losses of the mission, Bingham remarked that "the young princess, and a few others, were drawn into the snare of the devil, and occasioned disappointment and grief."

As the boredom of sanctified life under the missionary banner again weighed heavily on Nahienaena's spirit, she sought escape by going back to Honolulu with her guardian, Governor Hoapili. Richards, though reluctant to let her go, because he was well aware of the temptations awaiting her there, agreed to her request. But he lectured her for hours with a rehearsal of her failings, persuasions of prayer, and importunities for her good behavior, pressuring her until she wept in despair. By now she well knew the severe demands of Puritan Christianity as well as the opposite freedom of her traditional heritage. What she lacked, and none could offer her, was a sensible and discreet balance between the austerity of New England and the exhilaration of Hawaii.

Lorrin Andrews, a missionary who had come to Lahaina later, was even more denunciatory of the defects he claimed she was guilty of. He accused her of consorting with "every thief and whoremonger," persons her biographer believes were more likely "chiefs and chiefesses, companions, attendants, who enjoyed with her some of the mission-forbidden pleasures, people who did not press her with torrents of pious words or threats of damnation."

Nahienaena behaved quite seemly on Oahu, but the king was still indulging himself in his dissolute life style. In June he sought refuge in his country retreat and sent a ship to bring his sister to him. Disapproving his extremes of conduct, she refused to go. He attempted suicide.

Definite details of his actions never came to light. The missionaries just decided he had been drunk.

But the chiefs, who had long struggled over this national problem of their royalty, now acted to relieve this tragic affair. They resorted to the natural traditional solution of the situation. In the house of a high chief, Kauikeaouli and Nahienaena married according to ancient Hawaiian custom by sleeping together in the presence of the chiefs. A crier spread the news through the town. The missionaries were shocked.

When William Richards received the news in Lahaina, he conceived a way to touch the heart of the new queen. It was a dramatic gesture—writing her a letter from her mother's grave. The message and its meaningful source brought a flood of tears again to Nahienaena's eyes. But now she maintained her native rights and did not grant Richards the victory of making her yield.

Still, the royal pair were beset by conflicting pressures that their drinking could not alleviate. After six months, Nahienaena returned to Lahaina, not submitting to mission control but rather indulging herself in the ways they would forbid. She became so defiant in her ways that Andrews again gave vent to his violent disapproval by referring to her as "a drunken, hardened, incestuous apostate." Richards fought to force her to repent, finally by threatening excommunication. Now she did yield and submitted to their denial of her offensive pleasures. For in her heart lay respect for her mother, the missionary families, and the church whose tenets she had agreed to support.

Two years before, the missionaries and chiefs had sought another solution to her future by finding some suitable mate for her. But nothing came of their plans then. Before she had left Lahaina on her visit to Honolulu with her guardian, Hoapili, he with Richards and her had agreed on the selection of Leleiohoku, the ward of Governor Kuakini on Hawaii, as her husband. Now such arrangements were to be worked out for the marriage. She sailed to Kailua.

There, in the circle of native high society, she met her downfall. Reports came back from there that she was "guilty of intoxication and spent her nights in debauchery." Such, at least, was the missionary view. After two months of such life, she was formally excommunicated from her church on her return to Lahaina. But the church was willing to permit her royal wedding to be held there, and Richards performed the ceremony. Here again she became a ceremonial chiefess before the gaze of thousands of her people.

Missionary reports after that tell little of her life, except mentioning a trip to Honolulu when her brother was ill, until in early 1836 she was back on Maui, not in Lahaina but at Wailuku, where she had set up a residence sometime before. The missionary there was far from happy at her presence, calling her "wretched, polluted" and declaring she was "doing great mischief." A succeeding missionary, though disapproving her attitude and conduct, could better understand the inconsistencies of her nature. But one important part of her life at that time he did not realize. She was four months pregnant.

Her brother (ex-husband?), the king, came to take his sister to Honolulu for this royal birth. They spent three to four months together at Wailuku leading a "high life," according to one diarist. The newspaper report of September 17, 1836, records the birth of a son and his death a few hours later. Nahienaena lingered on in illness until the close of the year, dying on December 30.

Missionary wife Laura Judd, present at Nahienaena's death, passed down this account: "One of the bitter fruits of the king's irregularities was the corruption and apostasy of his royal sister, the once promising Nahienaena. For a while the tears and prayers of her beloved teachers, Mr. and Mrs. Richards, stayed the progress of evil in her, but the star that had shone with a brilliancy that delighted all beholders, was destined to go down in darkness.

"She forsook her old home and teachers, came to Honolulu, where she spent her last years in dissipation. I was by her bedside a little before she died. She was in great distress of mind, amounting to agony.

"'There is no mercy for an apostate. I am one,' she said. 'I have crucified the Lord afresh.'

"'Jesus spake pardon to the dying penitent on the cross,' I said.

"'Do you say so?' she exclaimed, clasping my hand. 'Can there be hope for one who has sinned as I have?'

"Then she made another effort to plead for mercy with that Saviour whose cause she had dishonored; but her strength failed—the golden bowl was broken."

Marjorie Sinclair questions whether "the zealous Mrs. Judd really heard those words,...or whether she indulged a kind of wishful fantasy of final repentance."

Bingham told that "efforts were made to lead her to repentence. . . She was induced to confess her sin and folly, and once more, in her distress, to call on the name of the Lord." But he was unsure of the success of the efforts.

As her body lay in state at the palace, her famous feather cloak was prominently displayed—"a symbol of her rank," remarks Sinclair; "and a symbol, ironically, which held connotations of the dilemma and anguish of her life."

And so she faded away, in Sinclair's words, "a plaything of history, a child of destiny."

XXV. The Persistent Power Of Pele

After the awful events following the death of Malama, Abner, "bedazed," suffers "in humiliation of spirit" and conjures up dire thoughts of vengeance on the place and people with "some awful Biblical destruction."

But he must contend with far worse demonstrations as Kelolo's precious goddess Pele proceeds to cause even greater trouble. She again appears to Kelolo, this time to warn him "of impending volcanic disasters."

Next morning the dire news arrives. Volcanic flows from Mauna Loa are threatening the town of Hilo. Noelani, the new Alii Nui, must hurry there to stop Pele's unrush and save the town.

And so she does: "Noelani planted her feet before the on-surging lava... and threw into [the advancing fires] tobacco, and two bottles of brandy which flamed furiously, and four red scarves, for that was the color Pele loved, and a red rooster and finally a lock of her own hair. And the fires of Pele...slowly froze into position. The flow of lava had halted at Noelani's feet."

❧ ❧ ❧

Missionaries, having keen curiosity and being interested in natural phenomena, delighted in exploring Hawaii's volcano region and became fascinated by the exciting eruptions. In their steadfast faith of God, they of course scorned any thought of a pagan goddess being responsible for such activities, supernatural though they be.

Charles Stewart acknowledged Pele to be "one of the most distinguished and most feared of the former gods" and accounted for her power as due to the volcano's "terrific features...well suited to the abode of an unpropitious demon...and...likely to impose thoughts of terror on the ignorant and superstitious, and...lead to sacrifices of propitiation and peace." But the missionary was pleased to report that this view was "now rapidly losing its power over the minds of the people." That was in July, 1825.

Pele had demonstrated her active support of Kamehameha in his campaigns of conquest by destroying in 1790 a section of his rival's army. In a rare heavy explosive eruption, pelting cinders and rocks with suffocating smoke and dust poured down upon some 400 men, women and children. The Footprints Trail at Volcanoes National Park offers the last bit of evidence of that tragedy.

First missionary explorations of Pele's realm on Hawaii were made by William Ellis with Asa Thurston, Artemas Bishop and Joseph Goodrich in their 1823 tour of the island. They did their best to free the natives from their fear of and belief in the terrible goddess, but Ellis, a good recorder of fact and fiction, faithfully put down some of the tales of Pele's legendary activities.

In a verbal contest Ellis had with a priestess of Pele, she refuted accusations that Pele had been destructive of the people. She declared that the rum and diseases of foreigners "have destroyed more of the king's men than all the volcanoes on the island." Ellis expressed his regrets for the diseases, assured her that Jehovah forbids intoxication, and duly warned her of her "'fearful doom" as an "idolatrous priestess," recommending she "cease to practice her deceptions."

After the missionary intrusion of the sacred precincts of Pele, another high priestess of the goddess appeared in Lahaina to protest against the desecrations by the foreigners who had invaded her domain and to demand that the chiefs send away these ruthless offenders. If not, "Pele would certainly...take vengeance, by inundating the country with lava, and destroying the people."

But the chiefs, regenerated from their ignorance and superstition, denounced her protestations as lies, declaring that volcanoes "are all under the control of the great God of Heaven." They made her confess she had been lying and admonished her, "Go home,...and deceive the people no more." Bingham was pleased at this "silencing of such an imposter."

Kapiolani Defies Pele

Bingham and Ellis and the other missionaries could exult more fervently at the dramatic success of "the missionary zeal" of one of their exemplary converts. Kapiolani had forsaken worldliness and tirelessly pursued the worship of God and spiritual conversations with the missionaries, winning their profound respect and admiration.

Bingham delineates her virtues: "She put on the costume of a Christian matron, and used chairs, tables and 'hospitality' in her habitation. Having a leading mind, an ardent heart, a portly person, black hair put up in a comb, a keen black eye, and an engaging countenance, Kapiolani, the daughter of King Keawemauhili, was vice-queen in the district assigned to her and her husband. They patronized the missionary, encouraged schools, and discountenanced iniquity, even threatening a fine for drunkenness. Their house of worship was thronged, and attentive hearers listened to the Gospel, and some were heard to inquire, 'What must I do to be saved?'"

With such fine credentials, Kapiolani, looking for greater fields to conquer, decided on a crusade to carry aid to the new Hilo mission, where Joseph Goodrich and Samuel Ruggles were "suffering privations" and struggling to overcome the strong local "superstitious reverence [for] the gods of the volcano, and other false deities." From Kealakekua on the west coast of the Big Island to Hilo on the east, the hardy Kapiolani tramped a hundred miles "by a rough, forbidding path" that lamed her with swollen feet.

Her spirit and determination never faltered. She pressed on to defy Pele on her own forbidden frontiers at Kilauea. A prophetess tried to block her way with warnings against approaching "the sacred dominions of Pele and predicted her death through the fury of the god, should she make an invasion with the feelings of hostility and contempt which she professed." But, when Kapiolani confronted her with readings from the Christian message, "the haughty prophetess quailed; her head dropped, and her garrulity ceased."

The arrival of Goodrich from Hilo heartened Kapiolani's purpose. The missionary, "who sometimes travelled barefoot," had hiked the 30 miles from Hilo to join and aid her at the Kilauea volcano, but Ruggles could not make it because he had been "for six months destitute of shoes."

Kapiolani, with Goodrich and her company of about 80, "descended from the rim of the crater to the black ledge. There, in full view of the terrific panorama before them, the effects of an agency often appalling, she calmly addressed the company thus: 'Jehovah is my God. He kindled these fires. I fear not Pele. If I perish by the anger of Pele, then you may fear the power of Pele; but if I trust in Jehovah, and he shall save me from the wrath of Pele when I break through her tabus, then you must fear and serve the Lord Jehovah. All the gods of Hawaii are vain. Great is the goodness of Jehovah in sending missionaries to turn us from these vanities to the living God and the way of righteousness.'" Then, competing "with the terrific bellowing and whizzing of the volcanic gases," they raised their voices "in a solemn hymn of praise to the true God" and joined in prayer: "and the God of heaven heard."

In a final outburst of glorification, Bingham lauds her as she "tramples on...ancient Pele's powers, succors the missionaries in their toil and privations, and urges forward her countrymen to the victory over ignorance, superstition, sin, Satan and his legions."

The Awesome Wonders Of Pele

Titus Coan, the missionary who took up residence in Hilo in 1835, found great adventure in climbing Mauna Loa, the world's largest active volcano, and gazing in awed wonder at the terrific eruptions. In his first attempt in 1843, he and his missionary companion, the Reverend John Paris of Waiohinu, almost lost their lives in their final mad dash to reach the summit and observe at first hand "the yawning fissures where the crimson flood had first poured out."

Deserted by their Hawaiian companions in their energetic push to gain their grand objective, they had unconcernedly pressed on without their food and water supplies. Now at their goal late in the afternoon, they must rush back down, for they realized their suffering and peril. Below them lay five miles of heavy snow that had fallen the night before and 25 miles of rugged lava.

Hungry, thirsty, exhausted, they "ran, stumbled and fell...scaling ridges and plunging into rugged ravines, tearing our shoes and garments, and drawing blood from our hands, faces, and feet." Falling and rising, encouraging each other not to give up, they at last in the darkness of night reached their camp and companions. Safe at last, they fell to the ground, "called for water and food, and did not rise until near noon the next day." It took them three days of "hobbling on lame feet" to make the descent to Hilo.

It was 1852 when the mighty Mauna Loa burst forth again into a "roaring furnace" from which gushed a burning river down the lofty mountainside towards Hilo. The eruption was so intense that the seaport town was subjected to the constant roar, quivering of the earth and a nighttime brilliance that shone more than a hundred miles out to sea. This lasted for 20 days and nights.

All this provided another must-see challenge for Coan. For four days he with four natives struggled up through the dense forests before they came out into the open to behold the mountain "belching out floods of fire" with an awful roar from about 20 miles away.

Again Coan determined to make a desperate drive to gain his goal and so "pressed forward,...with an interest that mocked all obstacles"—such as ridges, gorges and sharp, jagged lava. His baggage-men could not get over a stretch of intolerably sharp lava. The guide, with Coan's wrapper and blanket, later lagged behind. His missionary companion, Dr. Charles Wetmore, who had started out with him, had hurried back the third day for fear the rushing lava stream might reach the town and his services would be needed there. Now Coan stood at the "awful crater," 10,000 feet above the sea, "blinded by the insufferable brightness, almost petrified by the sublimity of the scene."

Coan reveled in all this magnificent spectacle. "I saw its gushings from the awful throat of the crater burning with intense heat. I saw the vast column of melted rocks mounting higher and still higher, while dazzling volleys and coruscations shot out like flaming meteors in every direction, exploding all the way up the ascending column of 1,000 feet...a thousand tons of the descending mass falling back into the burning throat of the crater."

Then, alarmed at being again alone in this dangerous vastness, he was relieved to see his guide making his way over the rough lava flow below. They spent the night there "within about 200 feet of the crater and watched its pyrotechnics, and heard its mutterings, its detonations, and its crashing thunder until morning."

They beheld "thousands and millions of tons of sparkling lava...pouring from the rim of the crater, while the cone was rising rapidly, and spreading out at the base. From the lower side of this cone a large fresh fissure opened, through which the molten flood was issuing and rushing down the mountain, burning its way through the forest."

This "river of liquid fire more than 40 miles long...came within ten miles of Hilo" in its 20-day run.

Only three years later, Mauna Loa released its fury in full blast for 15 months, from August, 1855, to November, 1856. Then, "the disgorgement of lava exceeded by millions of tons that of any other eruption" Coan had seen, he believed. Later estimates place the flow at 150 million cubic yards, compared to 250 million in 1843.

Watching the "deluge of liquid fire" rushing down toward Hilo, Coan waited seven weeks before he again set forth to watch the ravaging lava bursting its way through the forest. On the fifth day of their climb, Coan's party passed the forest area and found themselves about ten miles up the lava flow. "Far down the mountain, terrible fires were gleaming, cutting down a mightly forest and licking up rivers of water. High above us raged a glowing furnace, and under our very feet a burning flood was rushing... perhaps to consume all Hilo."

Pushing on, he relates, "we were startled; a yawning furnace was before us—hot, sulphurous gases were rushing up..." Then, approaching carefully, they "saw the swift river of fire some 50 feet below,...rushing at white heat, and with such fearful speed that we stood amazed." They pressed forward to gaze at other openings up to 200 feet in length, deep within them "the lava torrent hurrying toward the sea."

Farther up, an even more stupendous spectacle came into view—"the burning river uncovered for almost 500 feet, and dashing down a declivity of about 20 degrees, leaping precipices in a mad rage." Above them, they stared into the tunnel, seeing "the fiery cataract leaping over a cliff some 15 feet high, with a sullen roar which was terrific." Along they scrambled to the original starting point of the eruption, at about the 12,000-foot elevation. All action had stopped at that point.

In spite of the their lack of water, because the natives had neglected to fill the gourds on the way, and their suffering from piercing winds and having to sleep on "hard and rough lava," they "endured cold and thirst until Monday morning," rather than break the missionary's repeated ex-postulations against "unnecessary labor on the Lord's day." Though Coan himself admits he "would not have deemed it wrong to go down the mountain on the Sabbath," he was afraid that, "as our natives are slow to discriminate and reason on points of religion,...multitudes in all parts of the islands" might misjudge him as failing to practice what he preached.

About two weeks after his return, Coan set off again. This time he and his men reached a flow about two miles wide and stretching about ten miles. They faced "a scene of marvelous brilliancy and beauty [with] thousands of pools, and active fountains and streams of lava [that] boiled and glittered and spouted." All night long they watched the fiery stream below them devour the forest, sending 70-foot trees crashing like thunder.

Back home, he watched the eruption keep right on. Again he "visited the scene of action," this time to take "several ship-masters and other gentlemen," besides his two eager daughters, for an overnight excursion now only 15 miles to the flow. The sight these newcomers beheld seemed overwhelming to them—the igneous stream boiling with raging fury as it hit a stream of water.

Still another overnight journey up Mauna Loa Coan made when the threatening lava flow had pushed to within ten miles of Hilo. There he watched the lava stream pouring over a 70-foot precipice "from 2 P. M. to 10 A. M. of the next day." During the ensuing weeks, he made about eight more trips.

"As the flood of consuming fire came nearer and nearer, the anxiety in Hilo became more intense," he recorded. The people kept nighttime vigils and looked for "places of refuge to escape the impending ruin. Every house near the lower skirt of the forest was evacuated, and all the furniture and animals removed to places of safety.... The devouring enemy was within seven miles of us, his fiery lines extending two miles in width. Already had it descended on its devastated track 50 or 60 miles,...and no human power could set up any barriers, or arrest the on-coming destroyer."

But pray they could and did. Coan declared, "I have never seen more reverent audiences than those that assembled on our day of fasting and prayer."

Just a few days after this, came the influx of volcano watchers—from a United States frigate and several whale ships, as well as some from Honolulu to witness the grand show. "It was a great muster," Coan saw; "the cavalcade of ladies and gentlemen included the commodore and his suite, lawyers, judges, sheriff, merchants, ship-masters."

Coan took the more daring ones two or three miles up to see the breadth of the main flow. The others followed a path cut by natives to a camp prepared for them. When Coan and his group got back to the camp at sunset, they found it "demoralized." Frightened by "the glowing fires...rushing down in volume," the viewers had "fled deeper into the forest."

The commodore had vaulted unto his horse and dashed madly to the shore. "The frightened ladies and children wandered,...bewildered in the forest," until finally at midnight the last stragglers were back in camp. "Most of them were so terrified that they could not be persuaded to approach nearer to the burning river; but those who were reassured and ventured to join the party of observation were well repaid," Coan assures his readers.

By daybreak the power of prayer was fulfilled. Coan could rejoice. "The flow ceased...and from that day the fearful flood did not come another foot toward Hilo...leaving a breastwork of indurated lava some 25 feet high across the whole terminus of the stream. But what is most marvelous...is...that for nine months longer...the great terminal furnace of Mauna Loan was in full blast, sending down billions of cubic feet of molton rock in covered channels, and depositing it near the lower end of the stream, but without pushing beyond its breastworks."

Is Hilo Doomed?

Coan did not get to climb Mauna Loa again to stand in awe at volcanic wonders. Though this mountain that forms such a towering backdrop for Hilo did erupt 13 times before late 1880, these were only summit outbreaks or flows in other directions, When the next big threat to Hilo finally did materialize, Coan was nearing his 80th year and regretted he was not 20 years younger.

Heavenward again shot the vast column of molten rock in November, 1880, from a point about 12,000 feet above sea level. Coan recorded: "Brilliant jets of lava were thrown high in the air, and a pillar of blazing gases mounted thousands of feet skyward." The first two flows again went off away from the Hilo target, but the third one aimed in that direction, dividing itself into several channels.

By June 1, 1881, the lava torrent advanced 50 miles down to within 5 miles of the town and pushed persistently on. Coan and his fellow townspeople trembled. "The outlook was fearful," they felt; "a day of public humiliation and prayer was observed, as during the eruption of 1855."

It looked as though Hilo was surely doomed this time. "Some...people were calm; others were horror-stricken. Some packed up their goods and sent them to Honolulu or elsewhere, and some abandoned their houses. Visitors to the stream were now frequent."

One stream heading toward the center of town hardened, but that only diverted the flow into another stream that "came rushing down...with terrific force and uproar [of] exploding rocks.... Hilo was... in immediate danger. The lava...advanced so rapidly that by the 30th of June it was not more than two and a half miles from us, threatening to strike" a section close to the home of the Coans.

On it pushed, from 100 to 500 feet a day. But the Coans made no move to leave their house. Came August 10. The dire threat lay scarcely half a mile from the homes of despairing citizens. And then, after nine months and five days of wondering, guessing, fearing and confusion, the people saw the action begin to abate. "The raging flood, the stream, the smoke, the noise of the flow were checked; and in a day or two the great red dragon lay stiffened and harmless upon the borders of our village. The relief was unspeakable."

Although Coan tells that Hilo was crowded with visitors coming from all parts of the islands, the only special one he mentions is "our Princess Regent, sister of the king." Not a word does he let out of the Hawaiian chiefess who valiantly confronted Pele and won credit for inducing the fire goddess to cease her rampaging toward the destruction of Hilo. Nor does this great evangelist ever deign to make the slightest reference to that heathen goddess. Less religiously constrained was the son of another missionary. Edward Hitchcock, living in Hilo at the time, wrote his mother in May, 1881,

"The lava flow still continues to flow, notwithstanding Father Coan has been up and interviewed Madam Pele!"

Did Princess Ruth Stop Pele?

Though the exact descent of Ruth Keelikolani became quite debatable as to whether she was truly the great granddaughter of Kamehameha I, she came to be legally accepted as such. She was a tremendous person, physically, facially, emotionally and vocally. Although brought up by Kaahumanu and Kinau, both determined Christians, she dismayed the missionaries by aligning herself with those heathen gods they so earnestly sought to discredit. Proud of her heritage, Ruth scorned the foreign influence and stuck fast to all that was truly Hawaiian, so much so that she refused to speak English, although she could.

Kings Kamehameha IV and V were her half brothers. She served as governor of Hawaii Island for 14 years. Hawaiians sympathized with her for her loss of her loved ones—her dear husband at age 22, three children, and finally her adopted son at 23. The people respected and admired her and accepted her as a faithful leader of their land.

So, when Hilo was so dreadfully threatened by Pele descending toward the town in 1881, who could more likely placate the destructive goddess than Princess Ruth? After all, the people had tried prayers to the white men's God without results. Off to Honolulu sailed a delegation to implore this powerful chiefess to hasten to Hilo and serve as the savior of her people there.

Travel for a massive 6-foot-tall, 400-pound woman was no simple matter. By steamer Ruth sailed to Kailua, Kona, where she had to be swung by a sling used for unloading cattle, just as the mammoth Malama had to be carried to and from ship in Michener's account.

From Kailua she had to make a hard 100-mile journey across the island to Hilo. Her faithful retainers managed to shove their royal burden unto a wagon to serve as her conveyance for the trip. But the pressure on the axle proved too ponderous and it snapped in two. Ruth snapped too at the rude people who dared to laugh at her mishap. Finally aboard another wheeled transport, she gradually covered the miles ahead with the poor horse pulling and strong men pushing the wagon.

Who would not be wearied by such a strenuous journey over this rough land? Princess Ruth must rest now and feed her mighty frame...So she ordered her bed and hearty quantities of food prepared. Nothing more was on her mind than to eat and sleep and refresh her body and spirit. The people waited, baffled and angry. Pele kept up her merry dance down the mountain. Hilo's peril grew more imminent.

Just what finally stirred Ruth into propitiatory action can not be determined. Newspapers under missionary influence ignored the tale. Later personal accounts dramatized the salvation of Hilo in differing respects. The common story is that she ordered the acquisition of all the red silk handkerchiefs available, and her man "bought out the town and got some 30 of them." Also the bottle of brandy she demanded. Other versions make her offerings a pig, white rooster and bottle of gin, or, making the ceremony strictly Hawaiian, ohelo berries, red lehua blossoms and a gourd of awa.

Again her men hoisted Ruth up on a wagon and she haughtily rode up toward the advancing lava flow. There they had to break down the side of the carriage to get her out. Boldly she strode toward the red hot fiery moving mass, "as if she were going to greet an old friend." She chanted and implored the goddess to refrain from further destruction of the land. She made her offerings—whatever they were.

Returning to her amazed following, she had her bed made up right there to spend the night not far from Pele's activity. Such aplomb could not go unrewarded. By morning Pele's efforts had ceased, and peace came to the anxious people. It had been an awe-inspiring exhibition of priestly power. Ruth had indeed proved herself the savior of her people. At least that is one side of the story that printed records of the day chose to ignore.

Newspaper accounts do report the Christian prayer meetings in Hilo's churches and the presence of the Princess Regent Liliuokalani (whom Coan also mentioned), then serving as ruler while her brother King Kalakaua was off making his record as the first monarch to become a circumnavigator. In her book, "Hawaii's Story," the later queen does mention that Princess Ruth was among other royalty who had preceded her to Hilo but refrains from any additional reference to her.

But she does give full credit to the success of the churches' religious efforts. As the people "lived in terror of losing life and property," the churches put on the prayer meetings, and Liliuokalani with her suite attended one. After that, in about a week, "the flow had been stayed, and the volume of lava was diminishing [and] the great danger was over," she wrote, adding, "Naturally, devout men remembered the days of fervent prayer, and said that God...had listened to the supplications of his people," and "delivered them from the threatened evil." Such was her conviction and that of many others.

And Pele Marches On

This timely hold-up of Pele certainly did not mean that she would not still be up to her old tricks. About five years she stayed quiet in her mighty Mauna Loa mansion and then kept breaking out 11 times in the following 47 years but not aiming towards Hilo again. Then, forgetful, angry or playful, she shot out flank eruptions for 42 days in 1935, again toward the town of Hilo.

This time modern measures were tried to save the Hilo area from severe damage. As a last resort in the 1881 affair, plans were ready to dynamite the threatening flow, but it stopped before that could be tried. Now it was decided to try bombing Pele's rapidly plunging torrent. The Army Air Corps marked its target with 300-pound bombs first, then followed up with 600-pounders. The red hot lava bolted high in fantastic fountains, then settled into the opened hole to rush away in a new direction. Pele withdrew her fire power.

Again in 1942 this means was used to restrain Pele. Fears for the fate of Hilo as Pele rolled merrily downward 15 miles during the first four days prompted this bombing attack. Besides, the goddess had shown her disdain for military rules by brightly illuminating the skies during the blackout to hamper any other possible Japanese attack on the islands. Again the 600-pound bombs, 16 of them, broke a new channel and diverted the flow. Pele's efforts fizzled out entirely nine days later. With extreme caution, the military censored any publication of the eruption news until eight days later. Surveying the effects of this procedure 38 years later, the U. S. Geological Survey found an unexploded bomb on the lava in 1980.

In 1983, Congress considered a bill that included construction of earthen walls to divert lava flows away form Hilo in case of an emergency.

Not only in her tremendous volcanic actions does Pele live on but she also still exists as a goddess in the minds of many. She appears to them as a warning before she spews forth her fire. She takes different forms—an enticing lady with red or golden hair or an old, wrinkled woman, generally with a white dog.

Reports of her appearing were not unusual when we came to Kona in the early 1960's. Pele had a way of disappearing like magic too. People told us of the tourist who met a lovely lady on the hotel lanai that led to the rooms. She asked for a light for her cigaret. He reached down to get his lighter, looked up, and she had vanished. Pele, of course! She would also airily vacate the back seat of a car in which she had been given a ride or a closed room in a locked house where she had been allowed accommodations.

Pele has her worshipers too. George Lycurgus, who developed the Volcano House, became famous for his method of courting Pele for her favors of putting on shows for visitors. He would just toss a quart of gin into the crater to get her to perform.

More spectacular was a modern priestess, who would fly from Oahu to make various offerings to her special goddess, whom she considered as like a guardian angel or Catholic saint. She claimed Pele had cured one of her sons, visited her, caused her body to ache before an eruption, and proved helpful in removing the bad luck or illnesses of others who asked her to make offerings to Pele for them.

Pele flared forth more than two dozen times from her Kilauea retreat in 1983 and 1984, putting on magnificent shows of national interest. To top such performances, she blew her top at Mauna Loa for a grand spring showing in 1984, again playfully scaring the wits out of some Hilo residents by rushing at them to within four miles of the higher homes. Then she began to spread out into other channels and gradually die down.

For days, the residents of Hilo worried, the government became actively concerned, and the whole country sympathized with the threatened citizens. Everything possible to save the city was considered. Three methods seemed possible but were rejected. The flow was too far up to cool it by spraying water on it. Building a barrier would take too long. Although the volcanologist specialist on Mauna Loa's activities believed that bombing the cone would naturally divert the flow, authorities were unwilling to try this means because its effects had not been proven. Also they were reluctant to offend certain strong-minded Hawaiians' beliefs that eruptions are sacred demonstrations of the fire goddess Pele.

The county mayor even asked Hawaiian leaders to make religious offerings to Pele in hopes of placating her, as some Hawaiians had blamed this eruption on the desecration of ancient sacred sites. A Bible-quoting Christian in a letter to the West Hawaii paper denounced offerings to Pele as "an abomination to the Lord God" and commanded Hawaiians to "get on their knees before Almighty God and beg forgiveness for their sins." This roused high-spirited Hawaiians to respond and accuse the writer of "ignorance, bigotry, intolerance and arrogance."

So Pele is an irrefutable part of Hawaii, certainly physically, and still to some spiritually.

XXVI. WHAT THEY WROUGHT

"Poor old dim-witted" and "wizened Abner Hale" dies alone in his graveyard while taking care of the graves of Jerusha and Malama. His is a pathetic end, as he still struggles to "erase the evils of heathenism," now among the immigrant Chinese, and unable to understand the changes in aims and attitudes of his rich children living splendidly in Honolulu. Them he rejects for having forsaken the ways of the Lord and married into other missionary families polluted with Hawaiian blood.

For Dr. Whipple he has only contempt and pity, "appalled at the ravages which years and success" have done to his former missionary partner, now devoted to "wealth and concern for a sugar plantation."

So, to the end, Abner maintains his steadfast alliance with his cherished biblical precepts of God, stubbornly refusing to adapt to new ways of thought and life.

🐾 🐾 🐾

Far more adaptable the real missionaries to Hawaii became. Even staunch, God-loving Bingham, with his sometimes denunciatory attitude, managed to win high respect and love for his accomplishments during his two decades in the service of the Lord in Hawaii. Then he could well rejoice that "the age of schools, of wholesome laws, of Bibles, of spiritual sacrifices, and revivals, had come." As he regretfully prepared to sail from Honolulu in 1840 because of his wife's poor health, he was pleased that "numbers of my people, with anxious looks and tender tears, came around, and the parting aloha was exchanged with the mutual desire and hope of meeting there again."

Though Hiram and Sybil Bingham did not get to return, Hiram II, born in Honolulu in 1831, came back to his native land from Boston in 1857 to help carry on the missionary goals to Micronesia and especially the Gilbert Islands, where he translated the Bible into Gilbertese.

The Binghams' youngest daughter, Lydia, also carried on in missionary work as the second wife of Titus Coan, stationed at Hilo.

At Kailua-Kona, the doughty Thurstons sacrificed themselves unstintingly in their work of instructing the native people, winning their admiration and love, as we have told.

Though they had their human weaknesses, the often maligned mission aries ventured forth with high aims of unselfishly sharing the blessings they themselves had enjoyed in their native land. So they willingly forsook the land and their good life there, and the families and friends they loved so dearly, to take to Opukahaia's people the glories of the American civilization they so heartily relished for themselves.

The personal stories in the many books by and about these missionaries abound in tales of true pioneer struggles, of hardy men and women devoted to saving a declining people and preparing them for their role in the new world thrust upon them since the discovery of the islands by Captain James Cook in 1778. These are tales of proud efforts, personal sacrifice, and the spirit of helpfulness that American history is proud to acclaim. Such was the spirit and superior strength and faith of those missionaries who took the American ideals to those far-away shores.

Other capable and devoted men came to the aid of the early pioneers. In all, the American Board sent out to Hawaii 12 companies with a total of 189 persons: 84 missionaries, including 52 ministers, 14 teachers, 9 physicians, 5 printers, 1 bookbinder, and 3 business agents, with 75 wives, 8 children, 10 women teachers, 12 natives. Of the 84 missionaries, 33 served to death or to the end of the supported mission in 1863, 23 of them until death or retirement; 32 of them devoted from 30 to 60 years of their lives, contributing in all about 1900 years.

With the fifth company came John and Ursula Emerson from New Hampshire in 1832 and established the mission at Waialua on the north shore of Oahu. John spent his last 35 years there, while Ursula held on for 22 years more, generously devoting her energies to administering to and cheering these people whom she loved. John, she noted, had served "not only as pastor and spiritual guide to the people, but also as school-teacher, doctor, farmer and mechanic, and this not for a few hundred, but for thousands."

His all-round proficiency was well recognized by one of his faithful servants, who pointed out that, though one of John's sons became a ranchman, two of them physicians, another a surveyor, and one a minister, John knew and did more than all five of the boys put together, practicing all their vocations and surpassing them all in his wide range of work. Then the man added gratefully that John "got close to us in our homes, teaching us how to live."

The missionaries indeed offered vast varieties of knowledge, interests, talents and temperaments, thus contributing in many different ways to the developing nation. Five of them resigned from the mission, feeling that God really needed them to save the struggling monarchy from ignorance and wrongdoing. William Richards became the king's "Chaplain, Teacher and Translator" in 1838 and gave the chiefs lessons in political economy. Dr. Gerrit P. Judd played a strong role in government, first as translator in 1842 and then serving on the Treasury Board, as Secretary of State for Foreign Affairs and as Minister of the Interior.

Both men, impelled by the threats and assaults made by foreign representatives and their warships, traveled abroad to induce the maritime giants, the United States, Britain and France, to guarantee the independence of the islands. Though these ambassadors obtained assurances, no positive agreement was signed to which all three nations would commit themselves.

Lorrin Andrews, who had established Lahainaluna Seminary, later served as judge in various courts and as secretary of the Privy Council. Richard Armstrong took over as Minister of Public Instruction. Edwin Hall took Judd's place during his absence abroad and then became director of the government press and editor of its newspaper.

When decimating epidemics of measles, whooping cough and smallpox brought in by foreign ships assailed the highly susceptible native people, it was the medical knowledge and strenuous efforts of the missionaries to protect them with vaccinations and proper care that saved thousands from untimely death.

Such are the vast accomplishments that the casual critic overlooks. These men of God had their human faults. Their strict religious beliefs sometimes blinded them to the real values of the Hawaiian culture and the wisest way to deal with those "heathen" people. But they brought a sense of decency to a land polluted by members of their own race of lesser culture, such men as made Robert Louis Stevenson feel he hated to be one of the "beastly" white men in these attractive Pacific islands. Stevenson concluded, "With all their deficiency of candour, humour, and common sense, the missionaries are the best and most useful whites in the Pacific."

Also acknowledging some "blight" they caused, Bradford Smith, offering a comprehensive story of the missionaries in his "Yankees in Paradise," declares, "No one except a very prejudiced observer could deny their achievements."

Another student of life and events in the Pacific wrote, "Non-Christians may grin at the efforts of missionaries among heathen. But the mission aries are the only influence for good in the islands, the only white men seeking to mitigate the misery and ruin brought by the white man's system of trade.... Traders and sailors, whalers and soldiers have been their [the peoples'] enemies."

Though some characters and events may be regrettable, the inevitability of United States control rested in the long line of American contributions to the progress of the people, the development of the country and the build-up of the national government. With pressing foreign influence always prevalent, the take-over of Hawaii was just the natural course of events—the way of the world. The missionaries implanted Christian virtues and American principles. Would some other country have done better?

The old Congregational missionary churches still carry on and stand as memorials to the devoted men and women who sacrificed themselves and accomplished so much to lay the foundations for the Hawaiian people that they might develop in this hazardous world with knowledge and under standing of their problems and how to cope with them. They represent the beginnings of American life with high principles in Hawaii.

TALES OF THE PACIFIC

JACK LONDON

Stories of Hawaii by Jack London
Thirteen yarns drawn from the famous author's love affair with
Hawai'i Nei.
$6.95   ISBN 0-935180-08-7

The Mutiny of the Elsinore by Jack London
Based on a voyage around Cape Horn in a windjammer from
New York to Seattle in 1913, this romance between the lone
passenger and the captain's daughter reveals London at his
most fertile and fluent best. The lovers are forced to outrace a
rioting band of seagoing gangsters in the South Pacific.
$5.95   ISBN 0-935180-40-0

South Sea Tales by Jack London
Fiction from the violent days of the early century, set among
the atolls of French Oceania and the high islands of Samoa,
Fiji, Pitcairn, and "the terrible Solomons."
$6.95   ISBN 0-935180-14-1

HAWAII

Ancient History of the Hawaiian People by Abraham
Fornander
A reprint of this classic of precontact history tracing Hawaii's
saga from legendary times to the arrival of Captain Cook,
including an account of his demise. Originally published as
volume II in *An Account of the Polynesian Race: Its Origins and
Migration,* this historical work is an excellent reference for students and general readers alike. Written over a hundred years
ago, it still represents one of the few compendiums of precontact history available in a single source.
$8.95   ISBN 1-56647-147-8

Hawaii: Fiftieth Star by A. Grove Day
Told for the junior reader, this brief history of America's fiftieth state should also beguile the concerned adult. "Interesting,
enlightening, and timely reading for high school American and
World History groups."
$4.95   ISBN 0-935180-44-3

A Hawaiian Reader
Thirty-seven selections from the literature of the past hundred years, including such writers as Mark Twain, Robert Louis Stevenson and James Jones.
$6.95   ISBN 0-935180-07-9

Hawaii and Its People by A. Grove Day
An informal, one-volume narrative of the exotic and fascinating history of the peopling of the archipelago. The periods range from the first arrivals of Polynesian canoe voyagers to attainment of American statehood. A "headline history" brings the story from 1960 to 1990.
$4.95   ISBN 0-935180-50-8

True Tales of Hawaii and the South Seas Edited by A. Grove Day and Carl Stroven
Yarns from the real Pacific by 21 master storytellers, including Mark Twain, W. Somerset Maugham, Robert Louis Stevenson, and James A. Michener. This anthology comprises some of the best nonfiction writing about the South Pacific.
$5.95   ISBN 0-935180-22-2

A Hawaiian Reader, Vol. II
A companion volume to *A Hawaiian Reader*. Twenty-four selections from the exotic literary heritage of the Islands.
$6.95   ISBN 1-56647-207-5

Kona by Marjorie Sinclair
The best woman novelist of post-war Hawai'i dramatizes the conflict between a daughter of Old Hawai'i and her straitlaced Yankee husband.
$4.95   ISBN 0-935180-20-6

The Wild Wind, a novel by Marjorie Sinclair
On the Hana Coast of Maui, Lucia Gray, great-granddaughter of a New England missionary, seeks solitude but embarks on an interracial marriage with an Hawaiian cowboy. Then she faces some of the mysteries of the Polynesia of old.
$5.95   ISBN 0-935180-30-3

Claus Spreckels, The Sugar King in Hawaii by Jacob Adler
Sugar was the main economic game in Hawai'i a century ago, and the boldest player was Claus Spreckels, a California tycoon who built a second empire in the Islands by ruthless and often dubious means.
$5.95   ISBN 0-935180-76-1

Remember Pearl Harbor! by Blake Clark
An up-to-date edition of the first full-length account of the effect of the December 7, 1941 "blitz" that precipitated America's entrance into World War II and is still remembered vividly by military and civilian survivors of the airborne Japanese holocaust.
$4.95   ISBN 0-935180-49-4

Russian Flag Over Hawaii: The Mission of Jeffery Tolamy, a novel by Darwin Teilhet
A vigorous adventure novel in which a young American struggles to unshackle the grip held by Russian filibusters on the Kingdom of Kauai. Kamehameha the Great and many other historical figures play their roles in a colorful love story.
$5.95   ISBN 0-935180-28-1

Rape in Paradise by Theon Wright
The sensational "Massie Case" of the 1930's shattered the tranquil image that mainland U.S.A. had of Hawaii. One woman shouted "Rape!" and the island erupted with such turmoil that for 20 years it was deemed unprepared for statehood. A fascinating case study of race relations and military-civilian relations.
$5.95   ISBN 0-935180-88-5

Mark Twain in Hawaii: Roughing It in the Sandwich Islands
The noted humorist's account of his 1866 trip to Hawai'i at a time when the Islands were more for the native than the tourists. The writings first appeared in their present form in Twain's important book, *Roughing It.* Includes an introductory essay from *Mad About Islands* by A. Grove Day.
$4.95   ISBN 0-935180-93-1

The Trembling of a Leaf by W. Somerset Maugham
Stories of Hawai'i and the South Seas, including *Red,* the author's most successful story, and *Rain,* his most notorious one.
$4.95   ISBN 0-935180-21-4

Hawaii and Points South by A. Grove Day
Foreword by James A. Michener
A collection of the best of A. Grove Day's many shorter writings over a span of 40 years. The author has appended personal headnotes, revealing his reasons for choosing each particular subject.
$4.95   ISBN 0-935180-01-X

Pearl, a novel by Stirling Silliphant

In a world on the brink of war, the Hawaiian island of Oahu was still the perfect paradise. And in this lush and tranquil Pacific haven everyone clung to the illusion that their spectacular island could never be touched by the death and destruction of Hirohito's military machine.

$5.95   ISBN 0-935180-91-5

Horror in Paradise: Grim and Uncanny Tales from Hawaii and the South Seas, edited by A. Grove Day and Bacil F. Kirtley

Thirty-four writers narrate "true" episodes of sorcery and the supernatural, as well as gory events on sea and atoll.

$6.95   ISBN 0-935180-23-0

HAWAIIAN SOVEREIGNTY

Kalakaua: Renaissance King by Helena G. Allen

The third in a trilogy that also features Queen Liliuokalani and Sanford Ballard Dole, this book brings King Kalakaua, Hawai'i's most controversial king, to the fore as a true renaissance man. The complex facts of Kalakaua's life and personality are presented clearly and accurately along with his contributions to Hawaiian history.

$6.95   ISBN 1-56647-059-5

Nahi'ena'ena: Sacred Daughter of Hawai'i by Marjorie Sinclair

A unique biography of Kamehameha's sacred daughter who in legend was descended from the gods. The growing feelings and actions of Hawaiians for their national identity now place this story of Nahi'ena'ena in a wider perspective of the Hawaiian quest for sovereignty.

$4.95   ISBN 1-56647-080-3

Around the World With a King by William N. Armstrong, Introduction by Glen Grant

An account of King Kalakaua's circling of the globe. From Singapore to Cairo, Vienna to the Spanish frontier, follow Kalakaua as he becomes the first monarch to travel around the world.

$5.95   ISBN 1-56647-017-X

Hawaii's Story by Hawaii's Queen by Lydia Liliuokalani

The Hawaiian kingdom's last monarch wrote her biography in 1897, the year before the annexation of the Hawaiian Islands by the United States. Her story covers six decades of island history told from the viewpoint of a major historical figure.

$7.95   ISBN 0-935180-85-0

The Betrayal of Liliuokalani: Last Queen of Hawaii 1838-1917 by Helena G. Allen

A woman caught in the turbulent maelstrom of cultures in conflict. Treating Liliuokalani's life with authority, accuracy and details, *Betrayal* also is tremendously informative concerning the entire period of missionary activity and foreign encroachment in the Islands.

$7.95   ISBN 0-935180-89-3

HAWAIIAN LEGENDS

Myths and Legends of Hawaii by Dr. W.D. Westervelt

A broadly inclusive, one-volume collection of folklore by a leading authority. Completely edited and reset format for today's readers of the great prehistoric tales of Maui, Hina, Pele and her fiery family, and a dozen other heroic beings, human or ghostly.

$6.95   ISBN 0-935180-43-5

The Legends and Myths of Hawaii by David Kalakaua

Political and historical traditions and stories of the pre-Cook period capture the romance of old Polynesia. A rich collection of Hawaiian lore originally presented in 1888 by Hawai'i's "merrie monarch."

$7.95   ISBN 0-935180-86-9

Teller of Hawaiian Tales by Eric Knudsen

Son of a pioneer family of Kauai, the author spent most of his life on the Garden Island as a rancher, hunter of wild cattle, lawyer, and legislator. Here are 60 campfire yarns of gods and goddesses, ghosts and heroes, cowboy adventures and legendary feats among the valleys and peaks of the island.

$5.95   ISBN 0-935180-33-8

SOUTH SEAS

Best South Sea Stories

Fifteen writers capture all the romance and exotic adventure of the legendary South Pacific, including James A. Michener, James Norman Hall, W. Somerset Maugham, and Herman Melville.

$6.95   ISBN 0-935180-12-5

Love in the South Seas by Bengt Danielsson
The noted Swedish anthropologist who served as a member of the famed Kon-Tiki expedition here reveals the sex and family life of the Polynesians, based on early ac counts as well as his own observations during many years in the South Seas.
$5.95   ISBN 0-935180-25-7

The Blue of Capricorn by Eugene Burdick
Stories and sketches from Polynesia, Micronesia, and Melanesia by the co-author of *The Ugly American* and *The Ninth Wave*. Burdick's last book explores an ocean world rich in paradox and drama, a modern world of polyglot islanders and primitive savages.
$5.95   ISBN 0-935180-36-2

The Book of Puka Puka by Robert Dean Frisbie
Lone trader on a South Sea atoll, "Ropati" tells charmingly of his first years on Puka-Puka, where he was destined to rear five half-Polynesian children. Special foreword by A. Grove Day.
$5.95   ISBN 0-935180-27-3

Manga Reva by Robert Lee Eskridge
A wandering American painter voyaged to the distant Gambier Group in the South Pacific and, charmed by the life of the people of "The Forgotten Islands" of French Oceania, collected many stories from their past—including the supernatural. Special introduction by Julius Scammon Rodman.
$5.95   ISBN 0-935180-35-4

The Lure of Tahiti selected and edited by A. Grove Day
Fifteen stories and other choice extracts from the rich literature of "the most romantic island in the world." Authors include Jack London, James A. Michener, James Norman Hall, W. Somerset Maugham, Paul Gauguin, Pierre Loti, Herman Melville, William Bligh, and James Cook.
$5.95   ISBN 0-935180-31-1

In Search of Paradise by Paul L. Briand, Jr.
A joint biography of Charles Nordhoff and James Norman Hall, the celebrated collaborators of *Mutiny on the "Bounty"* and a dozen other classics of South Pacific literature. This book, going back to the time when both men flew combat missions on the Western Front in World War I, reveals that the lives of Nordhoff and Hall were almost as fascinating as their fiction.
$5.95   ISBN 0-935180-48-6

The Fatal Impact: Captain Cook in the South Pacific by Alan Moorehead
A superb narrative by an outstanding historian of the exploration of the world's greatest ocean—adventure, courage, endurance, and high purpose with unintended but inevitable results for the original inhabitants of the islands.
$4.95   ISBN 0-935180-77-X

The Forgotten One by James Norman Hall
Six "true tales of the South Seas," some of the best stories by the co-author of *Mutiny on the "Bounty."* Most of these selections portray "forgotten ones"—men who sought refuge on out-of-the-world islands of the Pacific.
$5.95   ISBN 0-935180-45-1

Home from the Sea: Robert Louis Stevenson in Samoa, by Richard Bermann
Impressions of the final years of R.L.S. in his mansion, Vailima, in Western Samoa, still writing books, caring for family and friends, and advising Polynesian chieftains in the local civil wars.
$5.95   ISBN 0-935180-29-X

Coronado's Quest: The Discovery of the American Southwest by A. Grove Day
The story of the expedition that first entered the American Southwest in 1540. A pageant of exploration with a cast of dashing men and women—not only Hispanic adventurers and valiant Indians of a dozen tribes, but gray-robed friars like Marcos de Niza—as well as Esteban, the black Moorish slave who was slain among the Zuni pueblos he had discovered.
$5.95   ISBN 0-935180-37-0

A Dream of Islands: Voyages of Self-Discovery in the South Seas by A. Gavan Daws
The South Seas... the islands of Tahiti, Hawai'i, Samoa, the Marquesas... the most seductive places on earth, where physically beautiful brown-skinned men and women move through a living dream of great erotic power. *A Dream of Islands* tells the stories of five famous Westerners who found their fate in the islands: John Williams, Herman Melville, Walter Murray Gibson, Robert Louis Stevenson, Paul Gauguin.
$4.95   ISBN 0-935180-71-2

His Majesty O'Keefe by Lawrence Klingman
and Gerald Green
The extraordinary true story of an Irish-American sailing captain who for 30
years ruled a private empire in the South Seas, a story as fantastic and colorful as any novelist could invent. Vivid in its picture of Pacific customs, it is
also filled with the oddity and drama of O'Keefe's career and a host of other
major characters whose adventures are part of the history of the South
Pacific. Made into a motion picture starring Errol Flynn.

$4.95   ISBN 0-935180-65-6

How to Order

For book rate (4-6 weeks; in Hawaii, 1-2 weeks) send check or
money order with an additional $3.00 for the first book and $1.00
for each additional book. For first class (1-2 weeks) add $4.00 for the first book,
$3.00 for each additional book.

Mutual Publishing
1215 Center Street, Suite 210
Honolulu, HI 96816
Tel (808) 732-1709 Fax (808) 734-4094
Email: mutual@lava.net
www.mutualpublishing.com